THE END
REVELATION UNFOLDS

JEFF WICKWIRE

*Turning*Point Church Publishing

© 2016 by Jeff Wickwire

Published by *Turning*Point Publishing
10700 Old Burleson Road, Fort Worth, Texas 76140
www.tpcfamily.org

Printed in the United States of America

Book and Cover design by Amber Nowell

ISBN: 978-0-9766763-3-1

First Edition: February 2016

<u>Dedication</u>

To Cathy, my wife, lifelong co-laborer in the gospel, best friend, mother of my children, and truest Christian I've ever known.

CONTENTS

Introduction

I was initially introduced to The Revelation Of Jesus Christ in seminary. My Greek professor at that time required me to translate several of the chapters from Greek to English, which to me sounded like a command to jump to the moon! Little did I know that this challenging assignment would open up a whole new world, not only of the beauty of the Greek language, but of the awesome content of The Revelation.

The first time I taught John's incredible vision to my own congregation, I never dreamed the way the project would grow. Through the years my notes snowballed until it recently dawned on me there was enough there to justify a book.

I must confess up front that, because I never intended my teachings to reach this stage, I didn't bother to keep track of all my sources. As with most ministers, I am a bee that gathers from many flowers. Some quotes I can remember for attribution, and others I can't. I have done my best to track my sources and give credit.

That said, I am deeply indebted to Dr. Mal Couch, the Greek professor I mentioned, for his own passion for the Bible and particularly the Book of Revelation. His writings and the times we spent in wonderful conversation on the end-times were used of God to light a candle in my own soul. I also want to thank Dr. Jim Combs for his wonderful work, "Rainbows From Revelation," which proved a tremendous resource.

I pray as you read this book it will prove beneficial both as a tool in helping you piece together the Apocalypse, and that it will stir your heart with increased anticipation of the return of the heavenly Bridegroom, Jesus Christ!

CHAPTER ONE

The Glorified Messiah

T O THE BELOVED DISCIPLE JOHN IT CAME - THE REVELATION OF JESUS CHRIST.
The resurrected Jesus may have had this high honor in mind during a conversation he had with Peter. It is worth a fresh look.

Jesus said to the Apostle Peter a 3rd time:

John 21:17-24, NIV "[17]…Feed my sheep. [18]I tell you the truth, when you were younger you dressed yourself and went where you wanted; but when you are old you will stretch out your hands, and someone else will dress you and lead you where you do not want to go."

[19]Jesus said this to indicate the kind of death by which Peter would glorify God. Then he said to him, "Follow me!"
[20]Peter turned and saw that the disciple whom Jesus loved was following them. (This was the one who had leaned back against Jesus at the supper and had said, 'Lord, who is going to betray you?')

[21]When Peter saw him, he asked, 'Lord, what about him?' [22]Jesus answered, 'If I want him to remain alive until I return, what is that to you? You must follow me.'

[23]Because of this, the rumor spread among the brothers that this disci-

ple would not die. But Jesus did not say that he would not die; he only said, 'If I want him to remain alive until I return, what is that to you?'

[24]This is the disciple who testifies to these things and who wrote them down. We know that his testimony is true."

In these passages, Jesus predicted that John would live much longer than Peter. He is the only one of the 12 not martyred. In his older years, the aged Apostle was banished to a lonely island called Patmos for his witness.

Patmos was located in the Aegean Sea around 60 miles SW of Ephesus and 100 miles east of Athens. It was a tiny island, about 10 miles long and 6 miles wide, barren of trees and extremely rocky. In short, no vacation resort.

It was on this tiny island that John was enslaved in chains and forced to work the mines of the island with nothing but criminals. Because of John's connection to it, Patmos today is a destination for Christian pilgrimage. Visitors can see the cave where John is said to have received his Revelation (the Cave of the Apocalypse), and several monasteries on the island are dedicated to Saint John.

At the time of John's banishment he was around 92 years old. The early, fledgling church was experiencing vicious persecution. The lunatic emperor Nero had gone so far as to burn Christians in his garden as human torches and now Domitian was wreaking havoc with the church.

John's revelation came at a time of an anti-Christian state—the Roman Government—and a multitude of anti-Christian religions. The immediate intent of the Revelation was to provide encouragement that Jesus was Lord and in control, and as an evangelistic appeal to the lost.

The Revelation that God gave to Jesus came to John on just an average *workin'-in-the-coal-mines* kind of day. The Bible records that John was spiritually translated by the spirit of God. He was given a succession of visions so incredible that they've boggled the minds of thinkers throughout the ages.

The Revelation has reached far beyond John's day and has rolled down to the very end of time and into eternity. As we study this amazing book, we're going to see:

- Jesus Christ as Lord and Master of all history.
- Accurate prediction of rise and fall of world empires.
- Incredible cosmic battle between forces of light and darkness.
- Twenty-one terrible judgments falling on a Christ-rejecting world…
- An evil Anti-Christian/Anti-Christ society set up by the most dia-bolical, evil, wicked ruler to ever set foot on the world stage.
- The establishment of a one-world economy, 1-world religion, and 1-world political system.
- The total destruction of Anti-Christ and his world system.
- The worst war in the history of all mankind.
- The glorious return of Christ as the Lion of Judah.
- A thousand years of peace under the rule of Christ.
- A final, brief rebellion against Him.
- The final Great White Throne judgment of sinners.

Keys To Understanding The Revelation

The Revelation is not always chronological; that is, John will some-times jump from the future to the past, then back to the future.

For example, Jesus is born in Chapter 12, is exalted in Chapter 5, and is walking in the midst of His churches in Chapter 1.

The beast who attacks God's two witnesses in Chapter 11 is not brought into existence until Chapter 13.

John wrote as it came to him. The Revelation constantly uses the words "like" or "as" "appeared to be" or "something like." This is because John is grasping for ways to describe what he is seeing. So he uses pictorial language through the use of metaphors and similes.

For instance, if we were watching an Amtrak train speed by we might say something like, "It shot by me like a bullet." Or watching a fire-work display, we might say, "That skyrocket fell like a shooting star." John is a 1st century man describing 20th and 21st century events the best he can.

Why Should We Study The Revelation?

We should study The Revelation because it is part of the Bible. No story is complete without reading the last chapter. Revelation is the last chapter in God's book, describing how the beginning recorded in Genesis ends up.

Revelation brings a sense of urgency. Men must accept Christ *now* because Revelation events could begin at any time.

And most of all, there are a total of 66 books in our Bible, but only one of them promises a special blessing for those who read and keep the words contained in it - and that is the Book of Revelation.

Revelation 1:3 - "God blesses the one who reads the words of this prophecy to the church, and he blesses all who listen to its message and obey what it says, for the time is near."

LET'S BEGIN!

Revelation 1:1 "This is a revelation from Jesus Christ, which God gave Him to show his servants the events that must soon take place. He sent an angel to present this revelation to his servant, John."

REVELATION is from the Greek word *"apokalupsis"* (ap-ok-al'-oop-sis)" We get "apocalypse" from this word. But it doesn't mean universal destruction like our English word. It means "to bring to light what has been previously unknown because it was veiled."

The book of Revelation is not John's Revelation, but is "the revelation of Jesus Christ, which God gave Him to show His servants what must soon come to pass" (Rev.1:1).

So what God is doing with the Revelation is bringing out of hiding or out of cover things that had never been revealed before. It was given to show His servants (from the early church all the way to us) "things which must shortly take place."

The phrase MUST SHORTLY TAKE PLACE is a Greek expression meaning a rapidity of execution once it does begin; a domino effect. We are also going to notice that the number seven or multiples of seven play a prominent role. In Bible numerology, the number seven means "complete." Our first encounter with seven is found in Revelation 1:4,

"This letter is from John to the seven churches in the province of Asia. Grace and peace to you from the one who is, who always was, and who is still to come; from the seven-fold Spirit before his throne…"

The Lord Jesus is revealed as He Who was, is, and is to come. The seven spirits John references are seven different manifestations or attributes that flow from God's majesty to the Messiah. They are found listed in Isaiah 11:1-2,

"¹Out of the stump of David's family will grow a shoot—yes, a new Branch bearing fruit from the old root.
² And the Spirit of the Lord will rest on him—
the Spirit of wisdom and understanding, the Spirit of counsel and might, the Spirit of knowledge and the fear of the Lord.

Next, John describes in verse 7 the 2nd coming of Christ at the end of the ages:

Revelation 1:7, AMP - "Behold, He is coming with the clouds, and every eye will see Him, even those who pierced Him; and all the tribes of the earth shall gaze upon Him and beat their breasts and mourn and lament over Him. Even so [must it be]. Amen (so be it)."

This is a great example of how John jumps to the end of things before he begins the beginning. When Christ Jesus returns—which will be the final climactic event of history as we know it—those who pierced Him (the Jews), all tribes of earth (nations and peoples), will mourn, literally "beat themselves," over what they missed.

In verse 10 he says: "I was in the Spirit [rapt in His power] on the Lord's Day, and I heard behind me a great voice like the calling of a war trumpet…"

The voice he heard then instructed him:

"What you see, write in a book and send it to the seven churches …" (NLV)

Thank God He did! And you're holding the result in your hands. The 7 churches He names were near Patmos. John was but a row-boat away from their location in Greece.

Contrary to what some may think, these churches were not full of only believers. They were, like our churches today, comprised of imperfect bodies of people containing true believers and unsaved "professors," but not genuine "possessors."

Jesus sends the equivalent of a postcard to each of these churches with a warning to the lost, and correction and encouragement to the saved.

When John turned to see the source of the voice, he saw: "…seven golden lampstands, and in the midst of the lampstands [One] like a Son of Man, clothed with a robe which reached to His feet and with a girdle of gold about His breast." (Revelation 1:12-13, AMP)

The lampstand John mentions was a lamp holder with seven spiral extensions coming off it, each extension containing oil and a wick.

John's use of the phrase "SON OF MAN" has no article in the Greek. It simply reads "One like Son of Man." His description of the risen Son of God is awesome and stunning!

Revelation 1:13, NKJV says He was "…clothed with a garment down to the feet and girded about the chest with a golden band."

GOLD symbolizes deity in The Revelation.

This Golden Band was like a thick belt about his waist. The same thing is described by Paul in Ephesians 6: "Gird yourself with (the belt of) truth."

Then Revelation 1:14, NKJV records, "His head and hair were white like wool, as white as snow, and His eyes like a flame of fire…"

Remember the use of "like" and "as." John is using the word "like" to describe what he saw as best he could.

WHITE hair depicts wisdom.

FIRE pictures cleansing, purging, and purifying judgment. His eyes were cleansing, and His mere gaze had a purifying effect.

Then Revelation 1:15, NKJV says, "His feet were like fine brass, as if refined in a furnace, and His voice as the sound of many waters;"

BRASS OR BRONZE are used in scripture to symbolize strength.

And His VOICE, LIKE MANY WATERS, was commanding and awesome, like the sound of a mighty waterfall.

Then John notes that the risen, glorified Messiah is holding something: "He had in His right hand seven stars, out of His mouth went a sharp two-edged sword, and His countenance was like the sun shining in its strength." (Revelation 1:16, NKJV)

SEVEN STARS: *Stars* is from the Greek word *"asteros"* and they represented the seven churches to whom John was initially addressing the Revelation.

The TWO-EDGED SWORD that went out of His mouth depicts judgment, particularly when He returns to judge the world.

When John sees all of this, he faints. "And when I saw Him, I fell at His feet as dead..." (1:17, NKJV).

Jesus "laid His right hand" on John and said, "Don't be afraid. I am the first and the last." Then in verse 18 He assures John that He "holds the keys to death and Hades."

KEYS represent absolute control and authority. No longer is the devil in control of death and hell, but the resurrected Jesus now holds the keys! What comes next is important. THE KEY TO THE ENTIRE BOOK is stated in verse 19:

"Write the things which you have seen, and the things which are, and the things which will take place after this."

The glorified Messiah is informing John that he is about to be shown the future: "The things which will take place after this." NKJV

So we have in The Revelation the greatest book of prophecy ever written, straight from the mouth of the risen Savior Himself! The first chapter ends with a summation and explanation of the things John had just seen:

Revelation 1:20, NKJV - "The mystery of the seven stars which you saw in My right hand, and the seven golden lampstands: The seven stars are the angels of the seven churches, and the seven lampstands which you saw are the seven churches."

The seven stars were the angels (*angelos*--messengers) of the seven churches, and were either the pastors, or perhaps a literal angel commissioned to the churches.

The seven lampstands were the churches themselves. And as we're about to discover, the risen Messiah has a direct word for each of them!

CHAPTER TWO

Post Cards From The Edge

IN THE LAST CHAPTER WE SAW THE GLORIFIED MESSI-AH STANDING IN THE MIDST OF 7 LAMPSTANDS AND 7 STARS.

The STARS were the angels (*angelos*) or messengers of the churches (likely the pastors).

The LAMPSTANDS were the churches themselves—7 in all. Jesus is seen holding both the 7 stars and the 7 lampstands in His right hand. A two-edged sword comes out of His mouth—a picture of judgment when He speaks.

Now beginning with chapter 2, the risen Messiah addresses each of these 7 churches.

The first church John addresses is in Ephesus. It is *The Loveless Church.*

Founded by Paul, the Ephesian Church prospered under the dark shadow of Diana worship. To this congregation Paul sent his marvelous Ephesians epistle, emphasizing spiritual riches, the spiritual walk, and spiritual warfare.

The city of Ephesus was the manufacturing center for the statues of Diana, the goddess of sex. It was a city infected with deep immorality, existing off of temple prostitution and paganism. The church at Ephesus was surrounded by massive sexual perversion and personal temptation.

We notice that Jesus' first comments to them are positive:

Revelation 2:2-3 - "I know all the things you do. I have seen your hard work and your patient endurance. I know you don't tolerate evil people. You have examined the claims of those who say they are apostles but are not. You have discovered they are liars. ³ You have patiently suffered for me without quitting."

So, their pluses were hard work, patient endurance, intolerance of evil, discernment and patient suffering without quitting. But the Lord's next statements are strongly corrective:

Revelation 2:4-5 - "But I have this complaint against you. You don't love me or each other as you did at first! ⁵ Look how far you have fallen! Turn back to me and do the works you did at first. If you don't repent, I will come and remove your lampstand from its place among the churches."

Notice: They hadn't "*lost*" their first love, they had "*left*" their first love. What was their "first Love?" It was the principle of ministering out of love for Him.

History tells us that the Ephesian church did indeed eventually wither and die.

NUGGET: All ministry should flow out of love and devotion for the Lord Jesus; not for fame, money or power.

The 2ⁿᵈ Church is in Smyrna. It is *the Persecuted Church That Persevered.*

The city of Smyrna was one of wealth and greatness. Jesus assures them that He is aware of their oppression and poverty. He actually tells them that, in fact, they are wealthy in what truly matters. Knowledge of salvation is true wealth!
Their persecutions originated with false teachers that were rising up to oppose true Christianity. Jesus assures them:

"Don't be afraid of what you are about to suffer. The devil will throw some of you into prison to test you. You will suffer for ten days. But if you remain faithful even when facing death, I will give you the crown of life." (Revelation 2:10)

The TEN DAYS spoken of likely referred to the 10 terrible periods of persecution unleashed by the Roman Empire from about 64 to 316 A.D.

Jesus promised a "CROWN OF LIFE" to those that stayed true to the faith. This crown is one of 5 crowns listed in Scripture specifically promised for faithful obedience.

NUGGET: Jesus knows exactly what you're going through and what you will go through, and is there to strengthen and ultimately reward you!

The 3rd Church is in Pergamos. It is *The Lax, Compromising And Corrupted Church.*

Two false doctrines had crept into this church. The first is the doctrine of Balaam:

Revelation 2:14 "But I have a few complaints against you. You tolerate some among you whose teaching is like that of Balaam, who showed Balak how to trip up the people of Israel. He taught them to sin by eating food offered to idols and by committing sexual sin."

The Doctrine of Balaam refers to the advice of Balaam to Balak, the Moabite king, that encouraged the Moabites to intermingle and intermarry with the Israelites, resulting in God's judgment. In other words, the doctrine of Balaam was the doctrine of compromise, which always leads to corruption.

The second false teaching was the doctrine of the Nicolaitans. This doctrine encouraged sexual immorality, or what we would call hedonism with a spiritual twist.

In Revelation 2:15-16 Jesus warns them, "In a similar way, you have some Nicolaitans among you who follow the same teaching. [16] Repent of your sin, or I will come to you suddenly and fight against them with the sword of my mouth."

Halley's Bible Handbook tells us, "Sexual vice was actually a part of (Nicolaitan) heathen worship, and recognized as a proper thing in heathen festivals. Priestesses of Diana and kindred deities were public prostitutes.

In Ephesus, the Christian pastors, as a body, excluded such teachers. But in Pergamum and Thyatira, while we are not to think that the main body of pastors held such teachings, yet they tolerated within their ranks those who did."

NUGGET: It is the responsibility of every Christian to discern truth from error. And it clearly matters a great deal to Jesus what is taught in the church.

The 4th church is in Thyatira. It is *The Decadent Church That Drifted Into Darkness.*

Jesus's opening words tell a lot.

"This is the message from the Son of God, whose eyes are like flames of fire, whose feet are like polished bronze: [19] 'I know all the things you do. I have seen your love, your faith, your service, and your patient endurance. And I can see your constant improvement in all these things.'"(Revelation 2:18-19)

We can almost feel the penetrating, fiery eyes of the Son of God as He peers into this local assembly. And as with most of the other churches, there is a "But I have this complaint against you" involved.

Almost all of the Lord's message to Thyatira deals with a woman named Jezebel. This woman had introduced idolatry and immorality into the congregation. She was, according to Jesus in Revelation 2:20, "…leading my servants astray. She teaches them to commit sexual sin and to eat food offered to idols."

The act of bringing idolatry and immorality into the local church is soundly condemned by the risen Savior. He pronounces a sobering Word:

"I gave her time to repent, but she does not want to turn away from her immorality. [22] Therefore, I will throw her on a bed of suffering, and those who commit adultery with her will suffer greatly unless they repent and turn away from her evil deeds."

[23] I will strike her children dead. Then all the churches will know that I am the one who searches out the thoughts and intentions of every person. And I will give to each of you whatever you deserve" (Revelation 2:21-23).

But there is also a welcome promise delivered to Thyatira:

"But I also have a message for the rest of you in Thyatira who have not followed this false teaching ('deeper truths,' as they call them—depths of Satan, actually). I will ask nothing more of you [25] except that you hold tightly to what you have until I come. [26] To all who are victorious, who obey me to the very end, To them I will give authority over all the nations." (Revelation 2:24-26)

NUGGET: Jesus calls the practice of "normalizing sin" the "depths of Satan".

The 5th Church is in Sardis. It is *The Dead Church That Still Had The Lights On.*

Sardis was a very old city, wealthy in textiles and jewelry making. The city had a prostitution temple to Diana, as well as mystery cults. In these cults, emotional hysteria and bodily mutilation took place.

The Sardis church had a reputation for being alive, but actually they were spiritually dead. Jesus says of them:

"[1] I know all the things you do, and that you have a reputation for being alive—but you are dead. [2] Wake up! Strengthen what little remains, for even what is left is almost dead." (Revelation 3:1-2)

Even the little flicker of life they still had was in danger. Their external appearance covered up an internal dying condition. The Great Physician felt their spiritual pulse and pronounced them "dead."

They may have been a beehive of organized activity. Perhaps their reputation around town was one of being progressive, possessing a nice building, lots of money, and so on...but they were spiritually dead.

Jesus said they had "a name that lived." But "man looks on the outer appearance while God looks at the heart." Therefore, the glorified Savior, the Head of the Church, pierced through the facade and diagnosed their spiritual illness.

He did not find their works "perfect" before God, which means literally "finished" or "complete." They had not completed or finished their race, but had been sidetracked.

Jesus' command to them is clear and sobering: "[3] Repent and turn to me again. If you don't wake up, I will come to you suddenly, as unexpected as a thief." (Revelation 3:3)

NUGGET: While we may fool others, Jesus knows our true spiritual condition.

The 6th Church is in Philadelphia. It is *The Loving Church.*

The loving church (Philadelphia) proclaims the love of God.

Revelation 3:7 "I know all the things you do, and I have opened a door for you that no one can close. You have little strength, yet you obeyed my word and did not deny me."

Philadelphia is the only church in which Jesus finds no blemishes. He had opened for them a wonderful door of evangelism. Even those in Satan's synagogue would become convinced that their God was the true God.

Revelation 3:9 "[9] Look, I will force those who belong to Satan's synagogue—those liars who say they are Jews but are not—to come and bow down at your feet. They will acknowledge that you are the ones I love."

There is perhaps a hint of the Great Tribulation in verse 10: "Because you have obeyed my command to persevere, I will protect you from the great time of testing that will come upon the whole world to test those who belong to this world.[11] I am coming soon." (Revelation 3:10-

11)

A great time of testing coincides with the phrase great tribulation spoken of by Jesus:

"For at that time there will be such affliction (oppression and tribulation) as has not been from the beginning of the creation which God created until this particular time—and positively never will be [again]." (Mark 13:19 AMP)

One final exhortation from Jesus to the church at Philadelphia says:

"Hold on to what you have, so that no one will take away your crown (reward). ¹²All who are victorious will become pillars in the Temple of my God, and they will never have to leave it. And I will write on them the name of my God, and they will be citizens in the city of my God—the new Jerusalem that comes down from heaven from my God. And I will also write on them my new name." (Revelation 3:11-12)

The "names" Jesus says He will write on us suggest stamps of ownership. The believers in glory will wear, as it were, the name of God (relationship), the name of the New Jerusalem (citizenship), and the new name of Christ (ownership forever)!

NUGGET: With even a "little strength," much good can be done!

The 7ᵗʰ Church is in Laodicea. It is *The Lukewarm Church That Nauseates Christ.*

If one were to hold to the belief held by some that these seven churches are not only real churches in John's day, but also represent 7 historical phases the church would pass through before Christ's return, then Laodicea is certainly the church of the Last Days.

Some scholars believe that during the final stages of Christian history on this planet, there will be no great world-wide revival. Although powerful revivals could come in the end times, they will be localized. Lukewarmness is the end-time trait of professing Christians. Departing from the faith will characterize the last days Laodicean Church.

Jesus finds nothing in this church to commend. There is not one affirmation. Their lukewarm spiritual condition is utterly distasteful to the

Lord. According to the His message to this 7th church, Jesus would rather we be HOT or COLD in the spiritual sense. The Laodicean Church claimed wealth and prominence, but in God's sight they were in deep spiritual trouble.

Revelation 3:17 "[17] You say, 'I am rich. I have everything I want. I don't need a thing!' And you don't realize that you are wretched and miserable and poor and blind and naked."

Ever redemptive, Jesus advises them to buy "gold tried in the fire," and "eye salve" with which to anoint their eyes that they might truly see.

Gold represents the deity of Christ here. *Eye salve* represents spiritual illumination by the Holy Spirit.

These Laodiceans were seeing yet blind, rich yet poor, knowledgeable yet foolish. I personally believe that the church of today is the Laodicean church, the church of apostasy. So much of today's church has departed from the faith, particularly the belief in the deity of Christ, the infallible Word of God, and the importance of genuine righteousness and sincere godliness.

The church in much of the world (certainly the western church) has become focused on material riches, which is what characterized the Laodicean Church. Materialism had replaced true spiritual riches. May God help us to keep the flame of zeal lit, the fire of first love ablaze, and the oil in our lamps fueled with the moving of the Holy Spirit!

NUGGET: Lukewarmness is the pitfall end-time professing Christians should beware of.

Now that the Lord is finished addressing the churches, He is about to give John the trip of a lifetime as he calls the Apostle up into the sights and sounds of heaven!

CHAPTER THREE

John Sees Heaven

L AST TIME WE LOOKED AT THE 7 CHURCHES TO WHICH JOHN INITIALLY ADDRESSES HIS REVELATION TO. THEY WERE:

- 1st: Ephesus--Lacking
- 2nd: Smyrna--Loyal
- 3rd: Pergamos--Lax
- 4th: Thyatira--Loose
- 5th: Sardis--Lifeless
- 6th: Philadelphia--Loving
- 7th: Laodicea--Lukewarm

Now we come to Chapter 4 where John is caught up into the throne room of God. It should be noted at this point that many Bible teachers hold to the belief that verse 2, which records John being commanded to "come up here," represents the rapture of the church. However, the text doesn't say that. Such an interpretation must be read into it.

We do indeed find throughout the Revelation scenes in which vast multitudes are seen in heaven worshiping the Lamb, which must be the redeemed. But a clear cut description of the Rapture or "catching up" of the church is difficult to find. The various passages often cited by others seem somewhat forced. One event clearly described throughout the book is the Second Coming of Christ to the earth. And so John goes on to say:

"Then as I looked, I saw a door standing open in heaven, and the same voice I had heard before spoke to me like a trumpet blast. The voice said, 'Come up here, and I will show you what must happen after this.' ² And instantly I was in the Spirit…" (Revelation 4:1-2)

Notice: Verse 1 tells us that what John is about to see and hear is PRO-PHETIC in nature: "I will show you what must happen after this."

In chapters 4 and 5, an incredible drama now unfolds before John's eyes. He sees…

- The Absolute sovereign God over the affairs of men.
- The Absolute earthly Authority of Jesus the Messiah.
- The Providence of God in the coming World tribulation.

John is left totally speechless by what he witnesses! First, God is seen as a King on a throne.

Revelation 4:3 "The one sitting on the throne was as brilliant as gem-stones—like jasper and sardius. And the glow of an emerald circled his throne like a rainbow."

Three gemstones are mentioned:

Jasper: Is a clear crystal stone picturing purity.

Sardius: Is blood red stone, no doubt picturing the blood of the Lamb.

Emerald: Is light green stone, symbolizing majesty and royalty.

Next John notes: "Twenty-four thrones surrounded him, and twen-ty-four elders sat on them. They were all clothed in white and had gold crowns on their heads" (Revelation 4:4).

One explanation for the 24 elders is that they represent all of the re-deemed believers worshiping before God. In the O.T., the priesthood was divided into 24 divisions. In this church age, each believer is a priest before God.

The elders are all dressed in white, a picture of redemption. The crowns they wear picture rewards and authority. Since this is future and they are in heaven worshiping God, and that is our final destination, this explanation makes good sense.

Then next John notes,

"From the throne came flashes of lightning and the rumble of thunder..." (Revelation 4:5).

The lightning and thunder John experienced represent the awesome judgment and righteousness of the presence of God. The writer of Hebrews describes much the same thing regarding the appearance of God in the Old Testament.

"For you have not come to the mountain that may be touched and that burned with fire, and to blackness and darkness and tempest, 19 and the sound of a trumpet and the voice of words, so that those who heard it begged that the word should not be spoken to them anymore" (Heb. 12:18-19, NKJV).

Then John notes, "In front of the throne was a shiny sea of glass, sparkling like crystal..." (Rev. 4:6).

The SEA OF GLASS represents eternity. One of the most permanent substances to the ancients was glass. Everything else rusted, fell apart or eroded. God's sovereign throne room is eternal!

The amazed old Apostle goes on to describe,

"⁶...In the center and around the throne were four living beings, each covered with eyes, front and back. ⁷ The first of these living beings was like a lion; the second was like an ox; the third had a human face; and the fourth was like an eagle in flight. ⁸ Each of these living beings had six wings, and their wings were covered all over with eyes, inside and out." (Rev. 4:6-8).

The angelic beings John sees each have varied personalities

Many readers of the Revelation are thrown by John's descriptions of these beings. But one of the rules of Biblical hermeneutics (the science of interpreting the various types of literature found in the Bible) is that the Bible interprets itself. We compare Scripture with Scripture to find harmony and understanding of various Bible passages. Hence, the:

LION: represents authority

OX/CALF: meekness

MAN: intelligence

FLYING EAGLE: transcendent strength

SIX WINGS: moving swiftly, these are God's couriers doing His bidding and will.

Interestingly, we have a parallel of John's description in each of the four gospels. We find that in:

- Matthew, Jesus is presented as Christ, the Lion of Judah.
- Mark, He is emphasized as the humble servant.
- Luke, He is presented as the Perfect Man.
- John, His deity is stressed, symbolized by the flying eagle in John's vision.

John then notices in his vision,

"Whenever the living beings give glory and honor and thanks to the one sitting on the throne (the one who lives forever and ever), [10] the twenty-four elders fall down and worship the one sitting on the throne (the one who lives forever and ever). And they lay their crowns before the throne and say, [11] You are worthy, O Lord our God, to receive glory and honor and power. For you created all things, and they exist because you created what you pleased" (Rev. 4:9-11).

Thus, Chapter 4 concludes with a breathtaking worship session. Everything in heaven is praising God. And whatever men and angels have or receive from God, they will ultimately cast at His feet in praise!

As we come to chapter 5 the theme can be summed up in the words, WORTHY IS THE LAMB. As the awesome descriptions of the heavenly scenes continue, John records:

"Then I saw a scroll in the right hand of the one who was sitting on the throne. There was writing on the inside and the outside of the scroll, and it was sealed with SEVEN SEALS" (Revelation 5:1).

But then a predicament arises. There is no one found worthy to open the book and seals. Not one person in the universe can be found worthy! As if to magnify the reality of what John has already noted, he sees something else,

"And I saw a strong angel, who shouted with a loud voice: "Who is worthy to break the seals on this scroll and open it?" But no one in heaven or on earth or under the earth was able to open the scroll and read it." (5:2-3)

John is overwhelmed by the realization that not a single one of God's created beings could open the scroll. He confesses,

"Then I began to weep bitterly because no one was found worthy to open the scroll, or to look at it" (Revelation 5:4).

Right when it looks as if there is no solution, one of the 24 elders—a representative of the Redeemed Church—steps forward and says:

"...Stop weeping! Look, the Lion of the tribe of Judah, the heir to David's throne, has won the victory. HE IS WORTHY to open the scroll and its seven seals" (Revelation 5:5).

With bated breath, John describes what he sees,

"And I looked, and behold, in the midst of the throne and of the four living creatures, and in the midst of the elders, stood a Lamb as though it had been slain, having seven horns and seven eyes, which are the seven Spirits of God sent out into all the earth" (5:6, NKJV).

The implication is clear. Only Christ Jesus is qualified to oversee the end time judgments found in the mysterious scroll. Christ appears, not as the Lion, but as the Lamb of God, and takes the book.

Remember when I told you that John's Revelation is going to present several sets of 7's, which is the Bible number for completion?

The Lamb is described here as having, "…seven horns and seven eyes, which represent the sevenfold Spirit of God that is sent out into every part of the earth."

HORNS in the Bible are a symbol of power and strength. So Jesus's power is presented as perfect and complete.

The 7 EYES, which are The seven Spirits of God, symbolize perfect knowledge, God's omniscience. For instance, Zechariah 4:10 says, "…These seven are the eyes of the Lord which travel over all the earth."

And 2 Chronicles 16:9, KJ21 states, "For the eyes of the Lord run to and fro throughout the whole earth, to show himself strong in behalf of them whose heart is perfect toward him."

Then we see that within the scroll are 7 seals. These seals represent the beginning of God's awesome judgments on a Christ-rejecting world, and it starts in Chapter 6.

As with Chapter 4, Chapter 5 ends with an incredible worship session.

Revelation 5:8-14 – "[8] And when he took the scroll, the four living beings and the twenty-four elders fell down before the Lamb. Each one had a harp, and they held gold bowls filled with incense, which are the prayers of God's people. [9] And they sang a new song with these words:

"You are worthy to take the scroll and break its seals and open it. For you were slaughtered, and your blood has ransomed people for God from every tribe and language and people and nation.

[10] And you have caused them to become a Kingdom of priests for our God. And they will reign on the earth."

[11] Then I looked again, and I heard the voices of thousands and millions (literally, a vast angelic choir of one hundred million with thousands of thousands more) of angels around the throne and of the living beings and the elders.

[12] And they sang in a mighty (sevenfold acclamation of praise to the Lamb) chorus:

"Worthy is the Lamb who was slaughtered—

to receive power and riches
and wisdom and strength
and honor and glory and blessing."

[13] And then I heard every creature in heaven and on earth and under the earth and in the sea. They sang:

"Blessing and honor and glory and power
belong to the one sitting on the throne
and to the Lamb forever and ever."

[14] And the four living beings said, "Amen!" And the twenty-four elders fell down and worshiped the Lamb."

The Beginning Of The End

Chapter 5 has ended. Next, God's awesome judgments begin! Chapters 6-19 vividly describe and predict the Great Tribulation. The Great Tribulation occupies 14 of the 22 chapters of the book.

The Tribulation is also called "The Day of the Lord" in the O.T. It is the climactic era in God's plan for the ages. As with so much else in Revelation, the Great Tribulation contains several "7's." It will last exactly 7 years. And during those 7 years, God will pour out 3 sets of judgments, each consisting of 7 parts. They are called the 7 seals, the 7 trumpets, and the 7 bowls.

We are going to see that during the Great Tribulation, Satan, under God's permissive hand, is allowed to bring his evil forces to the earth, with the restraining hand of God no longer withholding his efforts. The Apostle Paul predicted this very thing:

2 Thessalonians. 2:3-6 "Don't be fooled by what they say. For that day will not come until there is a great rebellion against God and the man of lawlessness is revealed—the one who brings destruction. [4] He will exalt himself and defy everything that people call god and every object of worship. He will even sit in the temple of God, claiming that he himself is God. [5]Don't you remember that I told you about all this when I was with you? [6] And you know what is holding him back, for he can be revealed only when his time comes."

At this very moment, it is God who is holding back the appearance of

Antichrist. He will not arrive on the scene until his time has come.

THE 4 HORSEMEN OF THE APOCALYPSE

Chapter 6 opens with the appearance of the well-known four horsemen of the Apocalypse. These four horses represent four severe judgments that will be poured out upon a Christ rejecting world.

Revelation 6:1 "As I watched, the Lamb broke the first of the seven seals on the scroll. Then I heard one of the four living beings say with a voice like thunder, "Come!"

Remember the four living creatures around God's throne bearing the attributes of a lion, calf, man and eagle? The first one with the face of a lion has just cried out, "COME!" John then observes:

Revelation 6:2 "I looked up and saw a white horse standing there. Its rider carried a bow, and a crown was placed on his head. He rode out to win many battles and gain the victory."

Roman generals rode white horses. Most scholars believe this is the Antichrist. He will have authority depicted by the crown, but will conquer as the "good guy" at first.

British historian Arnold Toynbee said something worth quoting: "By forcing on mankind more and more lethal weapons and at the same time making the whole world more and more interdependent economically, technology has brought mankind to such a degree of stress that we are ripe for deifying any new Caesar that might succeed in giving the world unity and peace."

So, the rider of the white horse represents the arrival of the Anti-Christ. He looks noble, righteous, gallant. He will rise quickly to a place of prominence and will be hailed a problem solving genius for brokering a Middle East peace treaty. But he is the devil in disguise.

Then next the second creature with the face of a calf cries out:

Revelation 6:3-4 "After the LAMB breaks the second seal the second living creature with the attributes of a calf cried out, 'COME!' Then another horse appeared, a red one. Its rider was given a mighty sword and the authority to take peace from the earth. And there was war and slaughter everywhere."

The horse that follows testifies to the fact that Antichrist's peace is only temporary, for the next horse is the fiery red horse of war.

During the 20th century two major world wars engulfed the globe, involving dozens of nations and resulting in the deaths of millions. Yet midway through the Great Tribulation the world will be plunged into a conflict without parallel. With the release of this horse, the greatest war in the history of mankind will take place. It will culminate in the battle of Armageddon which, if not stopped by the return of Christ, would leave no flesh alive.

Jesus warned:

"For then there will be great tribulation (affliction, distress, and op-pression) such as has not been from the beginning of the world until now--no, and never will be [again]. 22And if those days had not been shortened, no human being would endure and survive, but for the sake of the elect (God's chosen ones) those days will be shortened" (Mat-thew 24:21-22, AMP).

Then John observes the third living being with the face of a man step-ping up...

Revelation 6:5-6 – "5 When the Lamb broke the third seal, I heard the third living being say, "Come!" I looked up and saw a black horse, and its rider was holding a pair of scales in his hand. 6And I heard a voice from among the four living beings say, "A loaf of wheat bread or three loaves of barley will cost a day's pay. And don't waste the olive oil and wine."

The black horse represents famine. Clearly, massive inflation is suggested here if one must work an entire day to pay for a loaf of bread.

John mentions oil and wine, which are luxuries, not necessities. Oil would represent our toiletries, beauty aids and body conditioners. The wine corresponds to the liquor that will be in abundance. It is possible that he is describing the total breakdown of a middle class. There will be a few rich, with the vast majority stricken with famine.

Today, one-percent of the American population has accumulated over 40% of the nation's wealth. This is a sign of the last times. Even now more than a billion people are on the brink of starvation. The reality is that out of 180 or so nations around the world, only 4—the U.S., Canada, France, and Argentina adequately feed their populous.

But after such a horrific war, famine will be even worse. When the red horse of war rides, the black horse of famine will be right on his heels!

Then finally, John sees the FOURTH SEAL broken and the fourth living creature with the face of an eagle cries out:

"When the Lamb broke the fourth seal, I heard the fourth living being say, "Come!" [8] I looked up and saw a horse whose color was pale green. Its rider was named Death, and his companion was the Grave. These two were given authority over one-fourth of the earth, to kill with the sword and famine and disease and wild animals." (Revelation 6:7-8)

The fourth horseman is called DEATH, and rides a pale horse. The Greek reads, *hippos chloros*—the word from which we get Cholera. The PALE HORSE is plague.

John has seen a stunning, sobering catastrophe. When this 4th horse rides, one-fourth of the earth's population will be wiped out in quick succession. This will happen with the sword (WAR), hunger (FAMINE), death (PESTILENCE), and with the beasts of the earth.

The worst plague in history was the Black Plague. It killed one-fourth of Europe in the 14th century. Over 25 million died. But two-thirds of the infected lived! It stopped after around a century.

But John predicts that a plague will come that will wipe out one-fourth of, not just Europe, but the entire world! As of July 2015, the world population was 7.3 billion. One fourth of that would be 1,825,000,000 people. Simply staggering.

It's possible that the pestilence will take the form of germ or biological warfare. It could even be nuclear. We don't know, only that it does indeed take place. All in all, during the release of these dreaded horsemen of the apocalypse, one out of every four human beings will die. This is a ghastly scene.

John has painted a chilling portrait of the closing of civilization. Keep in mind that these events are falling on a Christ rejecting, godless and unrepentant world. Amazingly, we will see later that not even these terrible judgments bring the end time world to repentance. They only double down on their blasphemies. Thank God, there is still time to respond to His amazing grace.

While the Apostle might have assumed it couldn't get much worse, it could. Cosmic catastrophes are about to unfold before his startled eyes.

CHAPTER FOUR

Cosmic Chaos

IN CHAPTERS 4 AND 5 WE WITNESSED AN INCREDIBLE DRAMA UNFOLDING BEFORE THE APOSTLE JOHN'S EYES. IT INCLUDED...

- The Absolute sovereignty of God over the affairs of men.
- The Absolute earthly Authority of Jesus the Messiah.
- The Providence of God in the coming World tribulation.

John is left totally speechless by what he sees! Then at the beginning of Chapter 6, we beheld the opening of the first 4 seals, and the dreaded 4 horsemen of the Apocalypse riding forth to destroy. But remember there were 7 seals, so we still have three to go.

When the FIFTH SEAL is opened, no longer do dreadful scenes on earth pass before us. The view shifts to heaven where an altar is seen. Let's look at what John sees:

Vs. 9-11, NIV "When he opened the fifth seal, I saw under the altar the souls of those who had been slain because of the word of God and the testimony they had maintained.

[10]They called out in a loud voice, "How long, Sovereign Lord, holy and true, until you judge the inhabitants of the earth and avenge our

blood?"

[11]Then each of them was given a white robe, and they were told to wait a little longer, until the number of their fellow servants and brothers who were to be killed as they had been was completed."

Just as the blood of sacrificial animals in O.T. times was poured at the bottom of the altar, so the souls of those who have given their lives for God are represented as under an altar.

In Chapter 7: 13-14, NIV we note that one of the elders around the throne asks, "...These in white robes—who are they, and where did they come from?"

And he is told, "These are they who have come out of the great tribulation; they have washed their robes and made them white in the blood of the Lamb."

Notice he didn't say "those who have come out of great tribulation." He uses the article and calls it THE Great Tribulation. So we assume here that these are people who come to Christ during the Great Tribulation.

We will see later that there will be 144,000 Jewish evangelists preaching the gospel during the Great Tribulation, so surely they will reap a great harvest of souls. Antichrist will see to it that multitudes of them become Tribulation martyrs.

These "Tribulation Saints" want to know how long it will be before their blood is avenged. They are told that others would also die before full vengeance is poured out on the persecutors, which will happen at the Return of Christ.

Then next John beholds COSMIC CATASTROPHES unleashed on the world with the opening of the sixth seal. When the SIXTH SEAL is broken, the scene shifts back to earth for a picture of the cataclysms, chaos and confusion which will befall much of the world at this stage of future history. These horrific events are occurring during the first half of the Great Tribulation.

6:12-13, NIV "I watched as he opened the sixth seal. There was a great earthquake. The sun turned black like sackcloth made of goat hair, the whole moon turned blood red, [13]and the stars in the sky fell to earth, as late figs drop from a fig tree when shaken by a strong wind. [14]The sky receded like a scroll, rolling up, and every mountain and island was removed from its place."

The earth, says John, will be violently shaken..."Every mountain and island was removed from its place." This passage confirms what Jeremiah the Prophet wrote long centuries before John:

"[23]I looked at the earth, and it was empty and formless.
  I looked at the heavens, and there was no light.
[24] I looked at the mountains and hills,
  and they trembled and shook.
[25] I looked, and all the people were gone.
  All the birds of the sky had flown away.
[26] I looked, and the fertile fields had become a wilderness.
  The towns lay in ruins,
  crushed by the Lord's fierce anger" (Jer. 4:23-26).

Isaiah the Prophet predicted the same world wide devastation:

"Therefore I will shake the heavens, and the earth will move out of her place, in the wrath of the Lord of hosts and in the day of His fierce anger" (Isa. 13:13, NKJV).

And again in Isaiah 2:19, NKJV he says, "They shall go into the holes of the rocks, and into the caves of the earth, from the terror of the Lord and the glory of His majesty, when He arises to shake the earth mightily."

This picture of men hiding amongst the rocks and in caves is exactly what John predicts in Rev. 6:16, which we'll read in a moment.

During the Great Tribulation, killer earthquakes will rock the planet. A world-wide blackout will occur as a result of volcanic and seismic disturbances when ash is spewed into the sky. And there will be an awesome reddening of the moon, as when a total eclipse occurs. Only here there is another cause. Even the Prophet Joel predicted "…the moon will be turned into blood…" (Joel 2:31)

This is not referring to the blood moons we've lately heard so much about. This will be a one time occurrence during the Day of the Lord.

Joel even says it will take place "Before the coming of the great and awesome Day of the Lord" (Joel 2:31, NKJV).

Jesus concurred in Matthew 24:29, NIV, saying, "Immediately after the distress of those days "'the sun will be darkened, and the moon will not give its light; the stars will fall from the sky, and the heavenly bodies will be shaken."

In addition, meteors, possibly asteroids and other interplanetary matter, slam into the earth. Unlike the ones we sometimes see streaking through the sky and disappearing, these will strike the ground.

"... Then the stars of the sky fell to the earth like green figs falling from a tree shaken by a strong wind." In other words, many of them are striking at once. The cosmic catastrophes are so bad that:

6:15-16 NIV "Then the kings of the earth, the princes, the generals, the rich, the mighty, and every slave and every free man hid in caves and among the rocks of the mountains." "They called to the mountains and the rocks, "Fall on us and hide us from the face of him who sits on the throne and from the wrath of the Lamb! [17]For the great day of their wrath has come, and who can stand?"

We must wait until Chapter 8 to see what the SEVENTH SEAL brings. Meanwhile, in chapter 7 we're going to make another visit into heaven with John as he again encounters the Tribulation Saints from Chapter 6.

Tribulation Believers

Revelation 7:1-4 NIV "After this I saw four angels standing at the four corners of the earth, holding back the four winds of the earth to prevent any wind from blowing on the land or on the sea or on any tree.

[2]Then I saw another angel coming up from the east, having the seal of the living God. He called out in a loud voice to the four angels who had been given power to harm the land and the sea:

[3]"Do not harm the land or the sea or the trees until we put a seal on the foreheads of the servants of our God." [4]Then I heard the number of those who were sealed: 144,000 from all the tribes of Israel."

John then names the 12 tribes and attributes 12,000 to each tribe.

You'll notice that between the 6th and the 7th seal, an interlude appears consisting of the entire chapter. It is a moment of pause as John is shown a vision of these 144,000 along with all of those who have been martyred during the Tribulation.

As John watches, a special sealing of the 144,000 takes place. We see them being sealed in their foreheads. This seal is like the seal of a notary on a document. It implies protection, legalization, authority and authenticity. Regardless of the winds of adversity, they will fulfill their ministry. These 144,000 will be the equivalent of 144,000 Jewish Billy Graham's, preaching the gospel throughout the world during the Tribulation.

Ironically, the false Christ—Antichrist—will also cause those submitted to his evil system to be marked on their foreheads with what John calls in a later chapter THE MARK OF THE BEAST. This mark also has a sealing effect, but for damnation, not salvation, for eternal loss, not eternal gain.

Clearly, these that are being sealed in Chapter 7 are Israelites, end-time Jewish people who accept Christ as Messiah and Savior during the Great Tribulation, becoming the "godly remnant" of the end times, and dynamic witnesses for the Lord.

During the first 3 ½ years of the Tribulation, they will be proclaimers of the gospel, spiritually and supernaturally protected while they spread the gospel. They will enjoy divine protection during this time period from the vicious attacks of Antichrist.

And John not only saw the 144,000, but also the fruit of their ministry:

[9]After this I looked and there before me was a great multitude that no one could count, from every nation, tribe, people and language, standing before the throne and in front of the Lamb. They were wearing white robes and were holding palm branches in their hands.

[10]And they cried out in a loud voice: "Salvation belongs to our God, who sits on the throne, and to the Lamb."

[11]All the angels were standing around the throne and around the elders and the four living creatures. They fell down on their faces before the throne and worshiped God, [12]saying:

"Amen!
  Praise and glory
  and wisdom and thanks and honor
  and power and strength
  be to our God for ever and ever.
Amen!"

[13]Then one of the elders asked me, "These in white robes—who are they, and where did they come from?"

[14]I answered, "Sir, you know."

And he said, "These are they who have come out of the great tribulation; they have washed their robes and made them white in the blood of the Lamb.

[15]Therefore, "they are before the throne of God and serve him day and night in his temple; and he who sits on the throne will spread his tent over them.

[16]Never again will they hunger; never again will they thirst. The sun will not beat upon them, nor any scorching heat.

[17]For the Lamb at the center of the throne will be their shepherd; he will lead them to springs of living water. And God will wipe away every tear from their eyes." (NIV)

This stunning description is of both Jewish and Gentile people who come to Christ under the preaching of the 144,000. Amazingly, one of the purposes of the Great Tribulation is to spark a world-wide revival. These multitudes dressed in white, worshiping before the throne of God are the result. People will get saved during the Great Tribulation, but most will die martyr's deaths.

The Seventh Seal

Next, in Chapter 8 we come to the dreaded 7th seal.

8:1 KJ21 "And when he had opened the seventh seal, there was silence in heaven about the space of half an hour."

This silence of half an hour has been called THE GREAT SILENCE. Up to now the Lamb of God has been engaged breaking the seals of the mysterious roll, which He only was worthy to touch or look upon. Six of the seals have been broken, but one yet remains. As that seal is broken there is a solemn expectancy seen rising in the angelic company looking on. All of heaven literally becomes mute at what is about to take place. John relays what follows:

2 "I saw the seven angels who stand before God, and they were given seven trumpets.

3 Then another angel with a gold incense burner came and stood at the altar..."

This "other angel" is no doubt the Lord Jesus Christ Himself. No other creature in heaven could answer prayers but Christ Himself, and we're about to see that the incense from the burner are the prayers of His martyred saints. Only the High Priest was allowed to make an offering on the brazen and golden altars, as we see taking place here in Chapter 8.

Verse 3 continues, "...And a great amount of incense was given to him to mix with the prayers of God's people as an offering on the gold altar before the throne."

The "prayers" John sees is the combined total of the cries of all martyrs and persecuted believers that have risen to the Throne Room of God, demanding justice. John says:

4 The smoke of the incense, mixed with the prayers of God's holy people, ascended up to God from the altar where the angel had poured them out."

Following this offering on the heavenly altar of incense and the prayers of God's people, cataclysmic events begin to take place on earth as God's wrath is poured out.

8:5 "Then the angel filled the incense burner with fire from the altar and threw it down upon the earth; and thunder crashed, lightning flashed, and there was a terrible earthquake."

Now, the thundering, lightning and earthquakes are only a prelude to what is about to take place. The 7 seals have now been broken and it's time now for the 2nd phase of God's judgments—the blowing of the 7 trumpets.

8:6 "Then the seven angels with the seven trumpets prepared to blow their mighty blasts."

Trumpets in Bible times signaled a time of solemnity or celebration. Trumpets were also associated with war, with assembling and marching, with festivals, with introduction of royalty, with the power of God, with overthrow of the ungodly, and with the coming of Christ.

These seven angels that stand in the presence of God, whose responsibility it is to sound the trumpets, appear to occupy a high and heavenly position. It is likely that the Archangels Michael and Gabriel are in their number. As they prepare to sound, the world's ecology is in view. And as we have seen so much happen in sevens so far, we are about to see some of God's judgments manifest in thirds.

THE FIRST TRUMPET

[7] "The first angel blew his trumpet, and hail and fire mixed with blood were thrown down on the earth. One-third of the earth was set on fire, one-third of the trees were burned, and all the green grass was burned."

There will be firestorms of incredible magnitude at the sounding of the first trumpet. John could certainly be describing a nuclear holocaust. A stunning 1/3 of the ground and trees are burned, and all of the green grass is destroyed. This is the beginning of the end of earth's ecology as we have known it.

THE SECOND TRUMPET

[8] "Then the second angel blew his trumpet, and a great mountain of fire was thrown into the sea. One-third of the water in the sea became blood, [9] one-third of all things living in the sea died, and one-third of all the ships on the sea were destroyed." (Revelation 8:8-9)

Again, this sounds an awful lot like a nuclear blast taking place at sea.

Our oceans are filled with submarines and ships armed with nuclear weaponry. So, while these verses perplexed believers of centuries ago, it is very easy for us to imagine such a catastrophe. It might also be the description of a giant meteor or comet streaking across the sky and plunging into the ocean.

Recent scientific speculations and calculations have pointed out the danger of an asteroid or a comet colliding with the earth, causing great catastrophes. In 1991 there was considerable concern among astronomers about an asteroid that came within a million miles of earth. Had it been captured by the earth's gravity, it could have fallen to earth.

With the 2nd trumpet, one-third of the sea becomes blood, a third of sea life is killed, and a third of the ships at sea are destroyed. This is truly a heartbreaking scenario in store for our planet!

THE THIRD TRUMPET

[10] "Then the third angel blew his trumpet, and a great star fell from the sky, burning like a torch. It fell on one-third of the rivers and on the springs of water. [11] The name of the star was Wormwood (bitterness). It made one-third of the water bitter, and many people died from drinking the bitter water."

When the third angel sounds, another great star burning like a torch falls upon earth. This is the second comet-like object to strike and contaminate the waters. John makes it clear that this time the springs, or fresh waters needed for drinking are struck.

Once again, let's keep in mind that John is a first-century man witnessing 21st century events. He is using the words "like" or "as" in his search for ways to best describe the horror of what he sees.

A "great star" falling from the sky could be anything. But since he called it "WORMWOOD" meaning "BITTER", one wonders about radioactivity from a nuclear exchange. People would indeed die upon drinking radioactive water.

THE FOURTH TRUMPET

[12] Then the fourth angel blew his trumpet, and one-third of the sun was struck, and one-third of the moon, and one-third of the stars, and they

became dark. And one-third of the day was dark, and also one-third of the night."

More than likely, because of the burning trees and grass, along with the ash and dust from such horrific explosions, the light of the sun, moon and stars is diminished by one-third. Keep in mind that it took the ash from Mt. Helen's eruption around ten years to leave the atmosphere.

Thus, the fourth trumpet completes the effect on the ecology; land, water and air. Unbelievably, these calamities and distresses, coming upon a planet embroiled in wicked wars, led by the coming Antichrist, are merely the preludes of even more intense woes.

Chapter 8 ominously closes with John seeing even worse on the way:

[13] "Then I looked, and I heard a single eagle crying loudly as it flew through the air, "Terror, terror, terror to all who belong to this world because of what will happen when the last three angels blow their trumpets."

CHAPTER FIVE

Demonic Terrors

LET'S TALK ABOUT GOD'S JUDGMENT.

The judgment of God is not a popular subject—even among Christians. A great majority of people abhor the thought that the "God of love" could also be the "God of wrath." But one cannot read the Bible without encountering the judgment of God.

In Genesis, God judged Adam and Eve, and doled out consequences for their sin. He judged the people of Noah's day with the great flood. The book of Jude informs us that He judged the angels that rebelled, reserving them in chains of darkness. And that He judged the people of Sodom and Gomorrah with fire from heaven (Jude 5-7). He even judged His own people who rebelled in the wilderness.

And in the Revelation, the full wrath of God is poured out on a Christ-rejecting, unrepentant world.

The holiness of God necessitates the judgment of God. A.W. Tozer writes, "God's first concern for His universe is its moral health. To preserve His creation God must destroy whatever would destroy it."

God is always fair and right in judgment because His nature is perfect. Abraham asked the rhetorical question just before God judged Sodom, "Shall not the judge of all the earth do right?"—Genesis 18:25

Jesus is Himself the Appointed Judge of all mankind: [22]Moreover, the Father judges no one, but has entrusted all judgment to the Son..."— John 5:22

God judges in order to place a restraint on evil. If He did not bring judgment on sin, the world would collapse into chaos. Yet the Lord prefers mercy to judgment: He is compassionate and long-suffering, "Not willing that any should perish but that all should come to repentance." (2 Peter 3:9, KJV)

Because judgment is often delayed in time (God is *long-suffering)*, many people assume He will never judge us. However when God does move in judgment He is thorough and even ruthless, as we see in the Revelation. With that in mind we come to the fifth trumpet.

THE FIFTH TRUMPET

"The fifth angel sounded his trumpet, and I saw a star that had fallen from the sky to the earth" (Revelation 9:1, NIV).

Two things about this star: First, it is a star that has *already fallen*. John is not watching it fall, but is noting that it has already happened. The language places this star in the masculine gender. So it is not an "it" but is a "he." John goes on to say:

Revelation 9:1-2, NIV "[1]The star was given the key to the shaft of the Abyss. [2]When he opened the Abyss, smoke rose from it like the smoke from a gigantic furnace. The sun and sky were darkened by the smoke from the Abyss."

Obviously, this star is Satan himself. When we first encounter the devil in Genesis, he is already a fallen creature. Jesus said, "...I saw Satan fall like lightning from heaven" (Luke 10:18, NIV).

Having been given the key to the bottomless pit, Satan opens it. The BOTTOMLESS PIT is the abode of demons, according to Luke 8:31. "The demons kept begging Jesus not to send them into the bottomless pit."

Rev. 11:7 says that Antichrist (the beast) also comes out of the bottomless pit. "When they complete their testimony, the beast that comes up out of the bottomless pit will declare war against them and he will conquer them and kill them."

So, the opening verse of Chapter 9 presents Satan as having the key to the pit of the abyss with power to release those who are confined there. And look what comes out of it!!

LOCUST CREATURES

Revelation 9:3-5 "³And out of the smoke locusts came down upon the earth and were given power like that of scorpions of the earth. ⁴They were told not to harm the grass of the earth or any plant or tree, but only those people who did not have the seal of God on their foreheads. ⁵They were not given power to kill them, but only to torture them for five months. And the agony they suffered was like that of the sting of a scorpion when it strikes a man."

As soon as the mouth of the awful pit is opened, a thick blackness issues from it like the black smoke of a great furnace. This blackness fills the air and obscures the sun. Out of the smoky blackness emerge creatures never before seen on earth; horrible in shape, evil in character, and armed with power to torment men's bodies without killing them.

Verse 6 says that "men will seek death and will not find it; they will desire to die, and death will flee from them."

The description of the locusts is bizarre:

Revelation 9:7-10 "⁷The locusts looked like horses prepared for battle. They had what looked like gold crowns on their heads, and their faces looked like human faces. ⁸They had hair like women's hair and teeth like the teeth of a lion. ⁹They wore a breastplate made of iron, and their wings roared like an army of chariots rushing into battle. ¹⁰They had tails that stung like scorpions, and for five months they had the power to torment people."

The symbology in John's description is striking:

- Locust
  Unrelenting
  Destruction
  Ruin

- Horses
  Strong
  Powerful
  Fearful in combat
- Crowns of Gold
  Attractive
  Possessing authority
- Faces of Man
  Intelligent
  Willful beings
- Hair of Women
  Attractive
  Disarming
- Teeth of a Lion
  Overpower
  Destroy
- Breastplates of Iron
  Indestructible – The breastplates of iron in the ancient world were considered to be the best piece of defensive equipment. This indicates that they cannot be defeated, and the only defense against them is fellowship with the Lord.
- Sound of Chariots
  Frightening, overpowering. The noise going into battle is awesome, which paralyzes their victims with fear before the attack is made.
- Tails of Scorpions
  Inflicting massive, painful torment.

John calls these creatures locusts but they are supernatural. Unlike the former plagues that decimate the earth's ecology, these diabolical creatures only afflict men.

Revelation 9:11 goes on to say, "Their king is the angel from the bottomless pit; his name in Hebrew is Abaddon, and in Greek, Apollyon—the Destroyer."

Greek: Apollyon actually means *the exterminator*.

Hebrew: Abaddon means *destruction*.

As horrible as this is, it's still not over.

Revelation 9:12, KJ21 records, "One woe is past; and behold, there come two woes more hereafter."

THE SIXTH TRUMPET

As we come to the sixth trumpet we find four angels posted at the Euphratės River:

Revelation 9:13-14, KJ21 "[13]And the sixth angel sounded, and I heard a voice from the four horns of the golden altar which is before God, [14]Saying to the sixth angel which had the trumpet, 'Loose the four angels which are bound in the great river Euphrates.'"

Now remember that we said the events in Revelation are NOT chronological. It moves from seven seals to seven trumpets to seven bowls, but from time to time John will jump forward or go backward in order to focus on a particular event.

In Revelation Chapter 9, he jumps forward and talks about the Euphrates River, giving us a prelude to the full story that is covered again in Chapter 16. So keep in mind that what John begins in Chapter 9 he will pick up on again in Chapters 15 and 16.

The Altar and Four Horns

In verse 13 we're shown an altar with four horns constructed on its corners. A horn is always a sign of power. Recall that the altar is the place where the prayers of martyred saints are going up to God and they have power with God. God responds by releasing His righteous judgments.

In verse 14 John then sees four angels bound at the Euphrates River who have been prepared for an hour, a day, a month and a year. What a sovereign God we serve! If we were standing right now at the Euphrates River and could peer into the spirit world, we would see these mighty four angels awaiting their command from God. They await His perfect timing.

Why the angels are posted here is a mystery. The Euphrates River has always been a physical and psychological boundary between east and west. It is 1800 miles long, 750 feet wide and 30 feet deep. In chapter

16 we will see that a mighty angel will dry it up making way for a 200 million man army to cross from the far east. But John leaves no doubt as to the grim mission of the four angels in chapter nine.

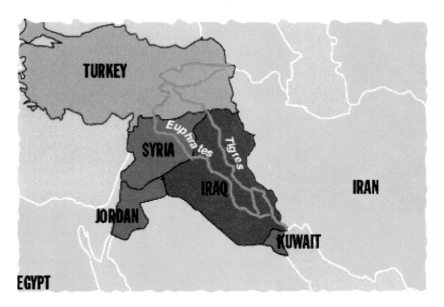

"15 And the four angels were loosed, which were prepared for an hour, and a day, and a month, and a year, for to slay the third part of men." (KJV)

When the sixth trumpet sounds, a third of human life will be destroyed. Heretofore it has been the ecology destroyed by thirds. But now it will be mankind. John describes the warriors this way:

Revelations 9:17, KJV "And thus I saw the horses in the vision, and them that sat on them, having breastplates of fire, and of jacinth and brimstone: and the heads of the horses were as the heads of lions; and out of their mouths issued fire and smoke and brimstone."

These are much like the colors used in desert camouflage, so that is one possible interpretation. Another might be modern day military helicopters equipped with nuclear weapons, which would account for "fire, smoke, and brimstone issuing from their mouths. This view might be further reinforced by John's next words:

Revelation 9:18-19, NKJV "18By these three plagues a third of mankind was killed - by the fire and by the smoke and the brimstone which came out of their mouths. [19]For their power is in their mouth and in their tails; for their tails were like unto serpents and had heads; and with them they do harm."

As for the camouflage colors held against what John described, we have the...

- Color of Fire--Red
- Jacinth or Hyacinth--Dull, dark blue
- Brimstone--Earth Yellow

Again, this is a first century man seeing 21st century things. John's description may depict cavalry weaponry, using fiery weapons of destruction, poison gas (smoke), and "brimstone," which can be a description of colossal explosive power, such as nuclear bombs. Many of the countries identified by Scripture now possess nuclear capability and the unleashing of it on the Asian continent could end in the slaughter of over a billion people.

We next encounter one of the most amazing and sad sights in all of the Word of God. In spite of all of the calamity, all of the obvious judgments of God, all of the terror and uncertainty, men still refuse to repent!

Revelation 9:20-21, KJV "[20]And the rest of the men, which were not killed by these plagues, yet repented not of the works of their hands, that they should not worship devils, and idols of gold, silver, brass, stone, and wood, which neither can see, nor hear, nor walk: [21]Neither repented they of their murders, nor of their sorceries, nor of their fornication, nor of their thefts."

It's hard to imagine a world more spiritually dark. Two words from John's sad description jump out.

SORCERIES: *Pharmakia*—drugs or use of drugs. The last days world will be a wash in drug abuse.

IDOLS: of gold, and silver, and brass, and stone, and of wood, which neither can see, nor hear, nor walk. We tend to think of idolatry as an Old Testament thing, but it's not. John saw it as extremely prevalent at the end of time. Remember, an idol is anything that takes the place of God in our lives--sex, drugs, some person, a career...these and much more can serve as idols that we worship.

It might interest you to know that at least one half of the world is idolatrous. All of India, three-quarters of Africa, great pockets of South and Central America, all of Asia including Japan, are practitioners of idolatry.

Time No Longer

As we come to chapter 10, we encounter a mighty angel holding a small scroll: "Then I saw another mighty angel coming down from heaven, surrounded by a cloud, with a rainbow over his head; His face shone like the sun and his feet were like pillars of fire." (Revelation 10:1)

As there was an interlude between the sixth and seventh seals in Chapter 7, Chapter 10 is an interlude between the sounding of the sixth and seventh trumpets. Chapters 10 and 11 are not only the middle of the book, but the middle of the seven-year Tribulation.

Many believe that the "mighty angel" in verse 1 is Christ Himself. His features closely parallel the description of the Glorified Christ of Chapter 1. John goes on to describe his actions:

Revelation 10:2-4 "²And in his hand was a small scroll that had been opened. He stood with his right foot on the sea and his left foot on the land. ³And he gave a great shout like the roar of a lion. And when he shouted the seven thunders answered. ⁴When the seven thunders spoke, I was about to write. But I heard a voice from heaven saying, 'Keep secret what the seven thunders said, and do not write it down.'"

While we do not know what the seven thunders said, it likely had to do with the horrendous future times of planet earth.

As we come to verses 5-7, the angel makes a stunning announcement--time as we have known it is about to end.

Revelation 10: 5- 7 "⁵Then the angel I saw standing on the sea and on the land raised his right hand toward heaven. ⁶He swore an oath in the name of the One who lives forever and ever, who created the heavens and everything in them, the earth and everything in it, and the sea and everything in it. He said, 'There shall be time no longer.' ⁷When the seventh angel blows his trumpet, God's mysterious plan will be fulfilled. It will happen just as he announced it to his servants the prophets."

And as noted earlier on, "7" is the Bible number for completion. As we draw near the blowing of the seventh trumpet, there is a growing sense that all things in God's timetable are about to be completed. The angel is informing John that time is about to be consummated. The end-time days, here designated as the "days of the voice of the seventh angel" indicates that the last half of the Tribulation will quickly occur. And much of it will revolve around the most important building in the world!

CHAPTER SIX

The Most Important Building In The World

IN THE LAST CHAPTER WE CLOSED OUT WITH A MIGHTY ANGEL, WHO IS LIKELY NONE OTHER THAN CHRIST Himself, descending from heaven. He is seen by John having one foot in the sea and another foot on the land. He announces that "time is no longer."

This event takes place mid-point through the Great Tribulation. History as we have known it is coming to a close. The end-time days, designated as the "days of the voice of the seventh angel," indicates that the last half of the Great Tribulation will quickly occur.

The mighty Angel holds in His hand a small book that has already been opened:

Revelation 10:8-11, NKJV "Then the voice which I heard from heaven spoke to me again and said, "Go, take the little book which is open in the hand of the angel who stands on the sea and on the earth." ⁹So I went to the angel and said to him, 'Give me the little book.' And he said to me, 'Take and eat it; and it will make your stomach bitter, but it will be as sweet as honey in your mouth.' ¹⁰Then I took the little book out of the angel's hand and ate it, and it was as sweet as honey in my mouth. But when I had eaten it, my stomach became bitter. ¹¹And he said to me, 'You must prophesy again about many peoples, nations, tongues, and kings.'"

Clearly, this mysterious little book contains the events about to be described. John is to literally ingest it, absorbing the information contained in the book into his mind and being.

Sweet are the promises and plans of God, but often the judgments and justice of God are bitter in results. What John is about to see taking place on earth is bitter indeed. In verse 11 is a prediction that John's Revelation would go to the entire world, as indeed it has!

The Rebuilt Temple

As we come to Chapter 11 it's important to note that from Chapters 11-14, John pauses in the chronological sequence of things to focus on some key events going on in the Tribulation. It's rather like a person driving 60 mph down a highway with little towns zipping by when their passenger says, "Slow down and take the next exit, let's drive around and see the sights."

Jesus is allowing us to see some close-up highlights of the first 3 ½ years of the Tribulation. First, he focuses on the end-time, rebuilt temple which is crucial to Tribulation. Revelation 11:1-2 says,

"Then I was given a measuring stick, and I was told, "Go and measure the Temple of God and the altar, and count the number of worshippers. ²But do not measure the outer courtyard, for it has been turned over to the nations. They will trample the holy city for 42 months."

Some Background On The Temple

When Abraham was told by God to offer Isaac, he went to the top of Mount Moriah. There, the drama of Isaac being spared by the intervening angel took place. Later, King Solomon ordered his engineers to literally cut the top off of Mount Moriah. In an amazing engineering feat they accomplished it in order to build the first glorious Solomonic Temple.

When the Jews were taken into Babylonian captivity, the glorious Temple was destroyed in 587 BC. Fifty years later, construction of a new temple was begun in 537 BC. After a 17-year hiatus, work resumed in 520 BC. The second temple was completed in 516 BC and dedicated in 515 BC.

So, 72 years after the first Temple was destroyed, it was rebuilt and dedicated. Five centuries later, this Second Temple was renovated by Herod the Great in about 20 BC. This was known as Herod's Temple. It was subsequently destroyed again by the Romans in 70 AD per Jesus' prediction:

"As Jesus was leaving the Temple grounds, his disciples pointed out to him the various Temple buildings. ²But he responded, "Do you see all these buildings? I tell you the truth, they will be completely demolished. Not one stone will be left on top of another!" (Matthew 24: 1-2)

The Jewish people were scattered at this time to the four corners of the earth, a people without a country, exactly according to Moses' prophetic forecast:

Deuteronomy 28: 64-67 says, "For the Lord will scatter you among all the nations from one end of the earth to the other. There you will worship foreign gods that neither you nor your ancestors have known, gods made of wood and stone!" "⁶⁵There among those nations you will find no peace or place to rest. And the Lord will cause your heart to tremble, your eyesight to fail, and your soul to despair. ⁶⁶Your life will constantly hang in the balance. You will live night and day in fear, unsure if you will survive. ⁶⁷In the morning you will say, 'If only it were night!' And in the evening you will say, 'If only it were morning!' For you will be terrified by the awful horrors you see around you."

Jewish history fulfills this prediction to a tee. There has never been a place or time in which the Jews were not persecuted, despised and rejected.

In the meantime, Islam was born around 700 A.D. Islam claims that at the end of his life, Mohammad rode into Jerusalem and ascended into heaven on a horse from the very spot where the Jewish Temple had been! The believers in Mohammad, the Muslims, eventually built a structure on that very spot and called it the Dome of the Rock. The Dome of the Rock has stood on the site of the Temple since the late 7th Century AD.

Now, meanwhile, God had promised through His prophets that the Jewish people would one day be restored to their homeland. Against all odds, after being relentlessly persecuted, despised, scattered and homeless, Israel became a nation again in 1948.

And in the famous 6-day war in 1967, they took the sacred city of Jerusalem again. Since that time the vitriol, hatred, war, and bloodshed between Arab and Jew has been unrelenting. The crux of the problem is that it is a battle over the land.

But let's be clear; there is no question that God gave that land to the Jewish people via Abraham, beginning all the way back to Genesis 12 in the covenant God made with him. Genesis 12:1 states, "The Lord had said to Abram, 'Leave your native country, your relatives, and your father's family, and go to the land that I will show you.'"

And Genesis 12:7 says, "Then the Lord appeared to Abram and said, 'I will give this land to your descendants.'"

All of this now brings us to Revelation 11: 1. "Then I was given a measuring stick and I was told, 'Go and measure the Temple of God and the altar, and count the number of worshippers.'"

This verse boldly predicts that the temple will again exist in the last days. You can't measure something that's not there. The Jewish people will build the temple again right where it used to be! This also presupposes that the old Jewish sacrifices and temple worship will be reinstated. John is told to "count the number of worshippers."

We will see in later chapters that the Antichrist will make a peace treaty with Israel. He will finally solve the age old Arab-Israeli conflict. No doubt one of the carrots he places in front of the Jews will be to allow them to practice their Old Testament rituals and worship!

But, though temple worship in Jerusalem will be restored, it will be interrupted once more by an invasion of Gentiles. Revelation 11:2 records, "But do not measure the outer courtyard, for it has been turned over to the nations (*ethnos*, the Greek word translated into ethnic groups). They will trample the holy city for 42 months (the 2nd half of the Tribulation)."

And who will these Gentile invaders be? The forces of Antichrist, who will dominate the Middle East and Jerusalem for 42 months, a period of 3 ½ years.

In summary, at the beginning of the Tribulation, Antichrist will make a peace treaty with Israel. The Prophet Daniel predicted, "The ruler (Antichrist) will make a treaty with the people for a period of one set of seven (seven-year peace time span)." No doubt about it, a peace pact between Arabs and Jews will finally be realized, but at the hands of Antichrist! Can you imagine the fame and adoration Antichrist will receive after solving a problem that has vexed the entire world for decades?

At the end of the first 3 ½ years, the Antichrist will stop the Jewish worship and Temple activities, and commit what Scripture calls "the abomination of desolation." The Prophet Daniel predicted:

Daniel 9:27 "The ruler will make a treaty with the people for a period of one set of 'seven', but after half this time, he will put an end to the sacrifices and offerings. And as a climax to all his terrible deeds, he will set up a sacrilegious object that causes desecration (the abomination of desolation), until the fate decreed for this defiler is finally poured out on him."

THE ABOMINATION OF DESOLATION

What is the "Abomination of Desolation"? In 167 BC a Greek ruler by the name of Antiochus Epiphanies set up an altar to Zeus over the altar of burnt offerings in the Jewish temple in Jerusalem. He also sacrificed a pig on the altar in the Temple in Jerusalem. This event is known as the Abomination of Desolation.

Jesus warned about a repeat of this:

Matthew 24:15 "The day is coming when you will see what Daniel the prophet spoke about—the sacrilegious object that causes desecration standing in the Holy Place. (Reader, pay attention!)"

It's important to keep in mind that in Matthew 24:15, Jesus was speaking some 200 years *after* the Abomination of Desolation described above had already occurred. So, Jesus must have been prophesying that some time in the future another Abomination of Desolation would occur in a Jewish temple in Jerusalem.

Revelation 13:14 eerily describes the Antichrist making some kind of image which all are forced to worship. Turning the Temple of the living God into a place of worship for the Antichrist is truly an "abomination."

For the first 3 ½ years, the new world leader will maintain warm and friendly relations with Israel, guaranteeing their integrity and autonomy. He will be a world-wide hero. Finally, the Arab-Israeli conflict will have been solved! But then he will break his treaty, invade Jerusalem, slay two witnesses (who we will look at next), and continue his evil domination for the final 42 months.

The important lesson to remember here is that you can't make a deal with the devil without getting burned!

Moses And Elijah Return?

John records that during the first 3 ½ years, the Antichrist will have a thorn in his side in the form of two witnesses who prophesy about the awesome judgments of God that are coming.

Revelation 11:3-6 "And I will give power to my two witnesses, and they will be clothed in burlap and will prophesy during those 1,260 days. [4]These two prophets are the two olive trees and the two lampstands that stand before the Lord of all the earth. [5]If anyone tries to harm them, fire flashes from their mouths and consumes their enemies. This is how anyone who tries to harm them must die. [6]They have power to shut the sky so that no rain will fall for as long as they prophesy (like Elijah did). And they have the power to turn the rivers and oceans into blood, and to strike the earth with every kind of plague as often as they wish (like Moses)."

Since it was Moses and Elijah that appeared to Christ on the Mount of Transfiguration, this is likely them again. Moses represents the law of God the world of that time will have utterly rejected. And Elijah represents the prophets whose warnings the world will also have thoroughly spurned.

When the Antichrist breaks his treaty with Israel and invades Jerusalem, the two witnesses are finally slain.

Revelation 11:7 "When they complete their testimony, the beast that comes up out of the bottomless pit will declare war against them, and he will conquer them and kill them."

Notice next how John uncannily predicts the ability of our present-day world to view something world-wide in real time, which can only happen via television or the Internet.

Revelation 11:8-9 "And their bodies will lie in the main street of Jerusalem, the city that is figuratively called "Sodom" and "Egypt," the city where their Lord was crucified. ⁹And for three and a half days, all peoples, tribes, languages, and nations will stare at their bodies…"

This passage alone mystified Bible scholars for centuries. "How could this be done?" they wondered. That is until the advent of satellite television and 24/7 news channels. This is just another of amazing proof that the Bible is a supernatural book, predicting times, events, and inventions millennia in the future!

Notice next how a world experiencing the Great Tribulation rejoices over the death of the righteous.

Revelation 11:9-10 predicts that, "…No one will be allowed to bury them. ¹⁰All the people who belong to this world will gloat over them and give presents to each other to celebrate the death of the two prophets who had tormented them."

But the world-wide celebration won't last long.

Revelation 11:11-12 records, "But after three and a half days, God breathed life into them, and they stood up! Terror struck all who were staring at them. ¹²Then a loud voice from heaven called to the two prophets, 'Come up here!' And they rose to heaven in a cloud as their enemies watched."

These two witnesses will be resurrected from the dead and caught up into heaven while the whole world continues to watch!

At the precise moment this happens, an earthquake will rock the city. Revelation 11:13 says, "At the same time there was a terrible earthquake that destroyed a tenth of the city. Seven thousand people died in that earthquake, and everyone else was terrified and gave glory to the God of heaven."

You might recall that God has sent signs via nature several times in Scripture in order to signify that something of high spiritual significance has taken place.

For instance, when Jesus hung on the Cross, the Bible says, "Now from the sixth hour until the ninth hour there was darkness over all the land" (Matthew 27:45, NKJV). And then when He died, Matthew records "... the earth quaked, and the rocks were split" (27:51, NKJV).

So it will be when these two God appointed witnesses are killed and resurrected. A great earthquake will rock Jerusalem. Next, John warns:

Revelation 11:14 "The second terror is past, but look, the third terror is coming quickly."

Remember how we said at the beginning of this series that the action often shifts from earth to heaven and back again. At this point in Chapter 11, John is taken up into heaven to witness the 7th angel blow his trumpet.

Revelation 11:15 "Then the seventh angel blew his trumpet, and there were loud voices shouting in heaven: 'The world has now become the Kingdom of our Lord and of his Christ, and he will reign forever and ever.'"

This last trumpet will encompass the entire time period of the final 42 months, described in detail all the way through Chapter 19. As we've already mentioned, this final 1,260 days is called, "the days of the voice of the seventh angel." (Revelation 10:7)

In heaven, John again sees the 24 elders representing all New Testament saints. They are rejoicing, worshiping, and proclaiming that the time of rewards in heaven is at hand. While at the same time, the hour of judgment on earth is in process.

Revelation 11:16-18 "The twenty-four elders sitting on their thrones before God fell with their faces to the ground and worshipped him. [17]And they said,

'We give thanks to you, Lord God, the Almighty,
    the one who is and who always was,
  for now you have assumed your great power
    and have begun to reign.

[18]"The nations were filled with wrath, but now the time of your wrath has come. It is time to judge the dead and reward your servants the prophets, as well as your holy people, and all who fear your name, from the least to the greatest. It is time to destroy all who have caused destruction on the earth."

Following this incredible scene, the remaining chapters of John's Revelation describe the conclusion of history. Civilization as we know it will destroy itself, and the Lord Jesus Christ will intervene in majesty and glory. Chapter 11 closes out with the tumult of lightning, thunder, an earthquake, and hail. More trouble for earth is on the way!

Revelation 11:19 "Then, in heaven, the Temple of God was opened and the Ark of his Covenant could be seen inside the Temple. Lightning flashed, thunder crashed and roared, and there was an earthquake and a terrible hailstorm."

CHAPTER
SEVEN

A Woman and a Dragon

LET'S SUMMARIZE OUR JOURNEY THUS FAR.

Chapters 1-3 in Revelation opened up with the Glorified Messiah appearing to John with a message to seven different churches.

Then, in Chapter 4, John is taken up into heaven and told that he is about to be shown things that will "soon take place" in the world.

In Chapter 5, a drama unfolds. A scroll with seven seals appears, but no one is found worthy to open it until the Lamb of God steps forward, who alone is worthy.

In Chapter 6, six of the seven seals are opened. The first four are the dreaded horsemen of the apocalypse that release the Antichrist, war, famine, and plague upon the earth.

Then the opening of the fifth seal reveals the souls of those who have been martyred, asking God how long before their lives are avenged.

The opening of the sixth seal releases cosmic catastrophes with the moon turning red as blood, the sun being obscured, and meteorite showers pummeling the earth.

John vividly records mankind's response to the heart stopping scene:

Revelation 6:15-17, NIV - "[15]…The kings of the earth, the princes, the generals, the rich, the mighty, every slave, and every free man hid in caves and among the rocks of the mountains. They called to the mountains and the rocks, 'Fall on us and hide us from the face of him who sits on the throne and from the wrath of the Lamb! For the great day of their wrath has come, and who can stand?'"

In Chapter 7, we saw 144,000 Jews, 12,000 from each of the 12 tribes of Israel, sealed by God to be witnesses during the Great Tribulation. We also saw a vast multitude no man could number of the redeemed worshiping God in heaven.

Chapter 8 reveals the seventh seal opened by the Lamb. A great silence falls upon the inhabitants of heaven, for the seventh seal portends the next series of judgments known as the seven trumpets.

The first four trumpets are blown in Chapter 8. With these fearsome trumpets, a third of earths ecology is burned up, a third of marine life is destroyed, a third of earth's clean water is turned bitter, and a third of the heavens is turned dark.

Chapter 9 sees the fifth trumpet blown, releasing demonic locust-like creatures that torment mankind for five months. The sixth trumpet then blows and four angels stationed at the Euphrates River are released to dry it up to make way for a massive 200-million man army to take part in the Battle of Armageddon. These are called the "kings of the east."

In Chapter 10, a mighty Angel, Who is likely the Lord Jesus Himself, stands with one foot in the sea and another on the land and declares that "time is no longer."

Then in Chapter 11, we observed two witnesses that prophesy in the streets of Jerusalem for the first 3 1/2 years of the Tribulation period. Midway through the Tribulation they are killed, but raised from the dead by God while the whole world watches. We also saw in Chapter 11 that the Temple will be rebuilt on its ancient site, even though what is now the Dome of the Rock occupies that spot.

Finally, in Chapter 11 the seventh trumpet sounds. This last trumpet releases a great worship session in heaven, and "flashes of lightning, rumblings, peals of thunder, an earthquake, and a great hailstorm," on earth.

Now let's process to chapter 12 and an amazing sight.

A Woman And A Dragon

As Chapter 12 opens, John has a "flashback" for the purpose of identifying and explaining the first of seven intriguing characters introduced in the end-times that we meet in both Chapters 12 and 13.

Revelation 12:1 "Then I witnessed in heaven an event of great significance. I saw a woman clothed with the sun, with the moon beneath her feet, and a crown of twelve stars on her head."

The "woman" John saw is Israel, both historical and as represented in Bible prophecy. From Genesis 37 and Joseph's dream, we see that the symbology of the "sun, moon and twelve stars" is clearly Israel.

Genesis 37: 9 "Soon Joseph had another dream, and again he told his brothers about it. 'Listen, I have had another dream,' he said. 'The sun, moon, and eleven stars bowed low before me!'"

How did Jacob interpret this dream?

Genesis 37:10 "...What kind of dream is that?' Jacob asked. 'Will your mother and I and your brothers actually come and bow to the ground before you?'"

Of course, Jacob and his twelve sons comprised the embryonic nation of Israel. The "great wonder" John saw was the "pregnancy" of Israel. But pregnant with whom?

Revelation 12:2 says, "She was pregnant, and she cried out because of her labor pains and the agony of giving birth."

Of course, this is none other than a symbolic picture of Israel (represented in Mary's pregnancy) bringing forth a "Wonder Child"—Christ Jesus the Lord. This is the ultimate fulfillment of the purpose for the Jewish race given to Abraham way back in Genesis 12:3 "And in you all the families of the earth shall be blessed."

A Chilling View Of Satan

Revelation 12:3 "Then I witnessed in heaven another significant event. I saw a large red dragon with seven heads and ten horns, with seven crowns on his heads."

The dragon is clearly the devil. Thirteen times in Revelation he's called a dragon. His seven heads depict the evil perfection of his influence on civilization's progress. And the ten horns are a prediction of the final alignment of Gentile world powers.

We will also see this seven-headed, ten-horned beast in later chapters depicting Antichrist's evil political system. Satan will work through a ten nation confederacy to enthrone his Antichrist as the world ruler.

Next, John is given a historical review of Satan's rebellion and fall prior to the Garden of Eden.

Revelation 12:4 "His tail swept away one-third of the stars (angels) in the sky, and he threw them to the earth…"

One third of the angels of God rebelled with Lucifer against God before the world was ever created. These fallen angels are the "principalities and powers" found in Ephesians 6 that we wrestle against in spiritual warfare. The record of this ancient Satanic rebellion against God is found in Isaiah 14:12-15; Ezekiel 28: 12-17.

A Vicious Attack

Next, as John looks on he sees a Satanic attempt to kill the child Jesus.

Revelation 12:4 "…He stood in front of the woman as she was about to give birth, ready to devour her baby as soon as it was born."

This is what took place through wicked King Herod when Jesus was born:

Matthew. 2:16-18 "[16]Herod was furious when he realized that the wise men had outwitted him. He sent soldiers to kill all the boys in and around Bethlehem who were two years old and under, based on the wise men's report of the star's first appearance. [17]Herod's brutal action fulfilled what God had spoken through the prophet Jeremiah: [18]'A cry was heard in Ramah—weeping and great mourning. Rachel weeps for her children, refusing to be comforted, for they are dead.'"

John's supernatural trip back through history continues as he witnesses the birth and victory of Jesus Christ:

Revelation 12:5 "She gave birth to a son who was to rule all nations with an iron rod. And her child was snatched away from the dragon and was caught up to God and to his throne."

Back to The Future

Next, John is transported back to the future as the narrative picks up 3 ½ years into the middle of the Great Tribulation. The new world ruler, the Antichrist, has severed his seven-year covenant with Israel, and slain the two witnesses in Jerusalem.

Now Israel, the woman, comes under persecution. Many Jews in that day will flee to "a place in the wilderness," perhaps even hundreds of thousands of those who still have not received Jesus as Messiah.

John says they will be protected for 1,260 days:

Revelation 12:6 "And the woman fled into the wilderness, where God had prepared a place to care for her for 1,260 days."

Now, yet another shift from earth to heaven takes place as John observes an incredible battle under way:

Revelation 12:7-9 "Then there was war in heaven. Michael and his angels fought against the dragon and his angels.""⁸And the dragon lost the battle, and he and his angels were forced out of heaven. ⁹This great dragon—the ancient serpent called the devil, or Satan, the one deceiving the whole world—was thrown down to the earth with all his angels."

While the Jews are in flight, Satan is totally expelled from heaven and denied even the limited access he now enjoys as revealed in Job, chapters 1 and 2. He is now confined primarily to earth for the final 1,260 days of the Tribulation. Heaven rejoices:

Revelation 12:10-12, NKJV "Then I heard a loud voice saying in heaven, "Now salvation, and strength, and the kingdom of our God, and the power of His Christ have come, for the accuser of our brethren, who accused them before our God day and night, has been cast down. [11] And they overcame him by the blood of the Lamb and by the word of their testimony, and they did not love their lives to the death. [12] Therefore rejoice, O heavens, and you who dwell in them! Woe to the inhabitants of the earth and the sea! For the devil has come down to you, having great wrath, because he knows that he has a short time."

The dragon is now filled with great wrath. How does that anger manifest itself? He proceeds to energize the Antichrist with supernatural power. Chapter 13 paints an incredible picture of how bad it becomes on the war-torn, sin infected, demon infested planet earth.

Revelation 13:5-6 "Then the beast was allowed to speak great blasphemies against God. Then he opened his mouth in blasphemy against God, to blaspheme His name, His tabernacle, and those who dwell in heaven."

Daniel the Prophet also predicted that the Antichrist would possess a vile, blaspheming tongue. He describes him as the "little horn" with "a mouth speaking pompous words" (Dan.7:8).

John continues with his description of this vile man Paul the Apostle calls "the man of sin," and "the son of perdition" (2 Thes. 2:3):

Revelation 13:7-8 "[7]And the beast was allowed to wage war against God's holy people and to conquer them. And he was given authority to rule over every tribe and people and language and nation. [8] And all the people who belong to this world worshipped the beast."

This is what the Bible calls "the time of Jacob's trouble" destined to come upon Israel. Satan hates Israel because they are God's elect, and because Israel (the woman John saw) gave birth to the Wonder Child— Jesus Christ! Satan releases his wrath on God's chosen people:

Revelation 12:13-14 - "When the dragon realized that he had been thrown down to the earth, he pursued the woman who had given birth to the male child. [14]But she was given two wings, like those of a great eagle, so she could fly to the place prepared for her in the wilderness. There she would be cared for and protected from the dragon for a time, times, and half a time."

Remember, many Jews in that day will flee to "a place in the wilderness," perhaps hundreds of thousands of those who still have not received Jesus as Messiah. John says they will be protected for 1,260 days:

Revelation 12:15-17 "Then the dragon tried to drown the woman with a flood of water that flowed from his mouth. [16]But the earth helped her by opening its mouth and swallowing the river that gushed out from the mouth of the dragon [17]and the dragon was angry at the woman and declared war against the rest of her children—all who keep God's commandments and maintain their testimony for Jesus." Satan hates all who name the name of Christ. This is likely a prediction of a flood of violent persecution.

The Appearance Of Antichrist

As we begin chapter 13, the Antichrist himself, the dreaded beast, steps onto the world stage. John records:

Revelation 13:1, NKJV "Then I stood on the sand of the sea. And I saw a beast rising up out of the sea, having seven heads and ten horns, and on his horns ten crowns, and on his heads a blasphemous name."

The phrase, "rising up out of the sea," is a description of how the Antichrist will rise out of the vast sea of humanity. The timeframe is still at the middle of the Tribulation.

Chapter 13 describes the "beast-king," who is elsewhere called the "Antichrist" (1 John 2:28, 3:3), the man of sin and son of perdition (2 Thessalonians 2:3-10), the little horn-king (Daniel 7: 8, 25), the prince that shall come (Daniel 9: 26-27), and the "abomination of desolation" (Matthew 15: 25).

The Antichrist is described as having "7 heads." John tells us later in chapter 17 that "...The seven heads are seven mountains on which the woman sits. [10]There are also seven kings..." (Rev. 17:9-10). The place of seven mountains is clearly Rome. And the kings he mentions are political rulers of a revived Roman empire. (More on this in chapter 17)

Then John also mentions seeing 10 horns. Again, in chapter 17, an angel explains to John what the ten horns represent. Let's take a peek.

"The ten horns which you saw are ten kings who have received no kingdom as yet, but they receive authority for one hour as kings with the beast. [13] These are of one mind, and they will give their power and authority to the beast. [14] These will make war with the Lamb, and the Lamb will overcome them, for He is Lord of lords and King of kings; and those who are with Him are called, chosen, and faithful" (Rev. 17:12-14, NKJV).

These ten horns likely represent ten nations that will join with the Antichrist in his attempt at world domination, as well as his attack against Christ and the tribulation saints. When I think of this ten nation confederacy, it seems highly probable that this will happen either through the United Nations or the European Union.

Again, we will visit this again when we come to chapter 17.

Antichrist's Personality

John next describes the diabolical personality traits of the Antichrist:

Revelation 13:2, NKJV "Now the beast which I saw was like a leopard, his feet were like *the feet of a bear*, and his mouth like the mouth of a lion. The dragon gave him his power, his throne, and great authority."

The animals used to describe him are characterized by the following:

LEOPARD: MOVES QUICKLY, STEALTH LIKE
BEAR: STRONG, POWERFUL
LION: ROARS AND IS KINGLY

John predicts that his kingdom will be strong and powerful, he will take over quickly (seemingly overnight), and he will be stately, ruling by the roar of powerful words.

The Antichrist at this time will be possessed of the devil like no other human being in the history of the world. Halfway through the Tribulation, he will commit the Abomination of Desolation we discussed earlier. He will walk into the rebuilt Temple, into the Holy of Holies, and will declare himself to be God. He IS the abomination that makes desolate!

It would appear that at this time an assassination attempt is made either on him, or on one of the kings associated with him:

Revelation 13:3 "I saw that one of the heads of the beast seemed wounded beyond recovery—but the fatal wound was healed! The whole world marveled at this miracle and gave allegiance to the beast."

Notice that the Bible says, "One of the heads…SEEMED wounded beyond recovery…"

Satan, the ultimate deceiver, would love to lead the world to believe that his Antichrist is resurrected just like Jesus was. I believe the Bible may be suggesting that it's a ruse. It only appears to be a literal resurrection.

The result of this "resurrection" is universal adulation:

Revelation 13:4, "They worshiped the dragon for giving the beast such power, and they also worshiped the beast. "Who is as great as the beast?" they exclaimed. "Who is able to fight against him?"

Antichrist is now at the height of his diabolical career. He leverages his popularity to commit pure evil. At the height of his wicked reign it seems as if nothing will take him down as he rides a crest of unprecedented popularity:

Revelation 13:5-9, KJV "⁵And there was given unto him a mouth speaking great things and blasphemies; and power was given unto him to continue forty and two months. ⁶And he opened his mouth in blasphemy against God, to blaspheme his name, and his tabernacle, and them that dwell in heaven. ⁷And it was given unto him to make war with the saints, and to overcome them: and power was given him over all kindreds, and tongues, and nations. ⁸And all that dwell upon the earth shall worship him, whose names are not written in the book of life of the Lamb slain from the foundation of the world. ⁹If any man have an ear, let him hear."

As Antichrist rides this wave of adulation, John warns that anyone trying to stop his reign of terror will be imprisoned or slain:

Revelation 13:10 "Anyone who is destined for prison will be taken to prison. Anyone destined to die by the sword will die by the sword. This means that God's holy people must endure persecution patiently and remain faithful."

The Antichrist will not conquer without the help of a second beast, a diabolical religious leader we're about to meet next.

CHAPTER EIGHT

Two Beasts and 666

IN THE LAST CHAPTER WE SAW WHAT JOHN CALLED "THE WOMAN" WHO IS ISRAEL AND THE JEWISH PEOPLE.

And we were also introduced to "The Dragon" who is none other than Satan himself. John describes how the dragon persecuted the woman, but she succeeded in bringing forth a "Wonder Child", Jesus Himself.

Chapter 12 concluded with Satan being cast from heaven and coming to earth in great anger. In his anger he empowers his Antichrist to do signs and wonders, and to seize control of much of the world. A persecution madness erupts in the final 3 ½ years of the Tribulation, where many of God's saints are martyred.

Then finally we witnessed at the beginning of chapter 13 the rise of Antichrist and several of his personal traits. He will take over quickly like a leopard, will be strong like a bear, and his oratory will roar like a lion.

The Second Beast

Next, John sees a second beast:

Revelation 13:11 "Then I saw another beast come up out of the earth.

He had two horns like those of a lamb, but he spoke with the voice of a dragon."

This second beast has horns like a lamb. Suggesting that he appears gentle and innocent. But he speaks under Satan's power with "the voice of a dragon." This is describing Antichrist's John the Baptist. He is obviously a religious leader of some sort, and his job is to point the world to the Antichrist. John goes on to describe him:

Revelation 13:12-13 "He exercised all the authority of the first beast. And he required all the earth and its people to worship the first beast, whose fatal wound had been healed.

[13] He did astounding miracles, even making fire flash down to earth from the sky while everyone was watching" (replicating the miracle of Elijah). Interestingly, for 2,500 years the Jews have longed for the coming of Elijah, primarily because Malachi prophesied his return: "Look, I am sending you the prophet Elijah before the great and dreadful day of the Lord arrives." (Malachi 4:5)

For the last 2,500 years Jewish families, when observing their annual "Passover" meal, have left a door or window open for Elijah to enter and join them in their anticipation of Messiah. Hence, this second beast will be the ultimate impostor! John continues:

Revelation 13:14 "And with all the miracles he was allowed to perform on behalf of the first beast, he deceived all the people who belong to this world. He ordered the people to make a great statue of the first beast, who was fatally wounded and then came back to life."

But a simple statue of Antichrist won't do. The second beast takes it a step further:

Revelation 13:15 "He was then permitted to give life to this statue so that it could speak. Then the statue of the beast commanded that anyone refusing to worship it must die."

For centuries, Bible students were perplexed as to how such a thing could be. But no longer. We now live in the age of animation. Statues can easily be made to talk, move, gesture, and so on. Even many pastors today have begun using hologram projectors, which create a 3-dimensional, life-like image of themselves without their having to be present. On entering the sanctuary, it is virtually impossible to tell that the image is not real.

Two-way television systems are now in place where the entire world could see a life-like image on their own computer screens, and be commanded to worship it. Not only would you see him, but even George Orwell in his book "1984" envisioned a system whereby *Big Brother* could also see you!

And we know that this also is now a reality. Many people I know put tape over the camera lens on their computer after confirmed reports that their computers could be hacked and their movements monitored. The second beast could quite possibly place this type of animated statue of the Antichrist in the Holy of Holies, commanding the world to worship him or suffer the death penalty.

At this point Antichrist doubles down and goes for what he's always wanted. The world is totally brought under his demonic domination. Worship Antichrist or die! This awful scene hearkens back to Nebuchadnezzar and the giant statue he made of himself. The whole kingdom of Babylon was ordered to fall down and worship it or be executed. Shadrach, Meshach and Abednego refused, and were thrown into the burning fiery oven. (See Daniel 3)

Major Changes Coming!

Next this diabolical "beast" duo bring the stakes even higher by forcing upon the world the infamous mark of the beast:

Revelation 13:16-17 "He required everyone—small and great, rich and poor, free and slave—to be given a mark on the right hand or on the forehead. [17] And no one could buy or sell anything without that mark, which was either the name of the beast or the number representing his name."

It is interesting that the Great Tribulation is accompanied by these kinds of identifying marks--either having God's mark or "seal" on your forehead as did the 144,000 Israelites we met in chapter 7, or you must take the devil's mark, which will be forced upon the Christ rejecting world. This technology is in place right now. It only awaits the right timing. For instance, a recent article was headlined:

Fingers Likely To Replace
ID cards in U.S.

The article reads, "Beginning in March, students at the University of California, Irvine were no longer required to show their ID cards to gain access to the Anteater Recreation Center. Instead, they only had to place their hands in a scanner and type in their personal identification numbers. (Future mark of the beast?)

Campus officials said the "hand geometry" system has been available for less than two months and almost 9,000 students have signed up to use it. With it, people no longer have to worry whether they have carried their ID or not. Their fingers are their IDs.[1]

This is only one example of the inexorable march toward the use of either a tiny implanted chip, or an invisible to the eye laser imprint on either the hand or forehead. Various things will drive this technology, credit card theft and identity theft at the top of the list.

There is little question that this "mark of the beast" prophecy will be implemented by technology that exists today; the biochip implant (syringe implantable microchip/lithium transponder), or an invisible tattoo designed to go in the right hand or forehead.

Cashless Society Coming

The mark of the beast John foresaw will usher in a world-wide cashless society. All financial transactions will be computer-generated. You will simply go to the supermarket, gather your groceries, and at the checkout counter a scanner will be swept across your hand or forehead. The money will then be withdrawn from your bank account. You will receive a receipt showing how much was removed and what you have left. Without this mark, you will not be able to buy or sell.

The move to a cashless society is gaining momentum as I write. In the USA, approximately 85% of all transactions are already cashless, and cash represents about 1-4% of bank deposits. Smart cards and biochip pet implants are now in wide use in Europe and America. In fact, in animal shelters it is now increasingly required that one must pay for a chip implant in order to adopt a pet. Are human beings next? The Bible says, yes.

---

[1] *www.chinaview.cn 2009-05-15*

Patrick Henningson of Global Research Company writes, "Right now we are now on the cusp of the US Dollar collapse, and perhaps a Euro implosion on the back end of it. Risks of hyper inflation are very real here..."[1]

Bill Gates of Microsoft fame is now promoting "digital currency" in third-world countries, which will make the poor even more dependent on central banks while also turning them into guinea pigs for the development of a "cashless society" in the U.S. and Europe.

Gates outlined his plan for a cashless society in a recently published letter in which he proposed the poor have better access to mobile phones so they can store their financial assets digitally instead of keeping hard currency. [2]

And the New York Times reports that "banks and retailers are trying to develop new payment systems using cell phones, and they're working on ways to protect customers' personal information. 'If we move to a truly cashless society, it won't be much of an adjustment for most Americans.'" [3]

Finally, Damon Darlin, again of the New York Times posits, "If I were to make a bet, I'd say that 10 years from now the most popular answer from young shoppers about how they make small payments would be: thumbprint. And you'll get a dull shrug when you ask what a wallet is." [4]

---

[1] *Patrick Henningson, Global Research website. 11/29/12.* [2] *Infowars website, Kit Daniels 1/22/15.* [3] *CBN News 9/28/14.* [4] *New York Times.*

A cashless society would be the IRS's dream, for it would give them knowledge and control over the finances of every American. But a world-wide cashless society would give control of the whole world's finances and personal information to none other than Antichrist!

666

John predicts that the mark of the beast will be a number:

Revelation 13:18 – "Wisdom is needed here. Let the one with understanding solve the meaning of the number of the beast, for it is the number of a man. His number is 666."

Again, for centuries no one really understood what this meant. That is, until computers came along. Now we know that the entire world could be marked by three sets of six digits each, much like a city of millions can all receive a phone number out of just ten digits—one through zero.

Prophecy expert Grant Jeffrey writes, "An enormous and sophisticated computer system in Europe will provide the initial consolidated financial integration of the economic systems of the advanced nations. Already an 18 digit number has been assigned to virtually every citizen of the western world. Your number includes your year of birth, sex, your current social insurance number, and a code identifying the street you live on."

While none of this is the Mark of the Beast system, it shows how close we are to the day when the diabolical Antichrist will seize the reins of power and utilize current technology to initiate his wicked plan of world control.

Using the amplified meanings of the original Greek text (sort of like the Amplified Bible, only in Greek), Michael E. O'Brien of highpraise. com created an expanded translation given of Revelation 13. Interestingly, it indicates a biochip implant containing a number like the social security number that could fulfill the prophecy very precisely.

Revelation 13: 16-18 - "[16] He [the second beast] caused everyone, small and great, rich and poor, free and slave, to receive an etching of servitude (made with a sharp point) in their right hand, or in their foreheads; [17] so that no one could buy or sell unless they had the etching of servitude, or the authority of the beast, or the number of his authority. [18]Here is wisdom. Let him that has understanding count the pebbles as the number of the beast, for it is an individual's [identification] number. His number is incised with a pricking action--willingly--by one claiming to possess the Godhead..."

John warns in no uncertain terms that the Mark of the Beast MUST NOT BE RECEIVED.

Revelation 14:9-10 - "[9]... Anyone who worships the beast and his statue or who accepts his mark on the forehead or on the hand [10] must drink the wine of God's anger. It has been poured full-strength into God's cup of wrath. And they will be tormented with fire and burning sulfur in the presence of the holy angels and the Lamb."

These warnings are likely directed at the Tribulation Saints. They must refuse the mark and trust God to provide for their needs.

Worship Unparalleled

Chapter 14 begins with John again taken into heaven, where once again he sees the 144,000 we first met in Chapter 7. They have the name of the Father on their foreheads.

Revelation 14:1 "Then I saw the Lamb standing on Mount Zion, and with him were 144,000 who had his name and his Father's name written on their foreheads."

This is the "seal" mentioned in Revelation 7:3. Now they are seen in heaven, for they likely die a martyrs' death when Satan, "the dragon," makes war with the "remnant" (Revelation 12:7).

Next, we witness an explosion of unparalleled worship.

Revelation 14:2 - "And I heard a sound from heaven like the roar of mighty ocean waves or the rolling of loud thunder. It was like the sound of many harpists playing together."

These majestic sounds are none other than the greatest choir ever assembled. It is the song of those who have been redeemed from the Great Tribulation. They are the fruit of the preaching of the 144,000. John seems to write ecstatically, "This great choir sang a wonderful new song in front of the throne of God and before the four living beings and the twenty-four elders. No one could learn this song except the 144,000 who had been redeemed from the earth." (Revelation 14:3)

Their personal walk of purity is particularly striking to the aged Apostle..

Revelation 14:4-5 - "⁴ They have kept themselves as pure as virgins, following the Lamb wherever he goes. They have been purchased from among the people on the earth as a special offering to God and to the Lamb. ⁵ They have told no lies; they are without blame."

This doesn't mean that they have never married, but that they are pure and holy through Christ and in their spiritual character, undefiled by immorality.

Six Angels

John next observes six angels, all with unique messages of warning and judgment. Let's begin by looking at the first three angels and their message.

FIRST ANGEL:

This angel's message is a gospel message--the "eternal good news."

Revelation 14:6-7 "6 And I saw another angel flying through the sky, carrying the eternal Good News to proclaim to the people who belong to this world—to every nation, tribe, language, and people. 7 'Fear God,' he shouted. 'Give glory to him. For the time has come when he will sit as judge. Worship him who made the heavens, the earth, the sea, and all the springs of water.'"

Think of it. Right in the middle of the most horrific time earth has ever seen, the mercy of God yet reaches out to the lost!

SECOND ANGEL:

This angel carries a message for Babylon.

Revelation 14:8 "Then another angel followed him through the sky, shouting, 'Babylon is fallen—that great city is fallen—because she made all the nations of the world drink the wine of her passionate immorality.'"

BABYLON represents the city, the system, and the regime of the final times. It is likely both a physical place and a spiritual condition of rebellion against God.

Babylon first appears in the Bible in Genesis 11, where we find Nimrod leading the charge in building the Tower of Babel, the Hebrew name for Babylon. God thwarted the effort and confused the people's languages. The Tower represented pride and rebellion against the will of God.

As for the place, ancient Babylon was located where present-day southern Iraq now is. The Bible predicts that Iraq will flourish and once again become a major city on the world stage. It could be that the Babylon John sees is that revived city where the infamous Iraq war has taken place. (We will look more closely at this in Chapters 17-18)

THIRD ANGEL:

This angel's message is a dire warning. Once again, God sternly advises against refusing the mark of the beast. To receive it is to perish eternally.

Revelation 14:9-11 "9 Then a third angel followed them, shouting, 'Anyone who worships the beast and his statue or who accepts his mark on the forehead or on the hand 10 must drink the wine of God's anger. It has been poured full strength into God's cup of wrath.

And they will be tormented with fire and burning sulfur in the presence of the holy angels and the Lamb. 11 The smoke of their torment will rise forever and ever, and they will have no relief day or night, for they have worshiped the beast and his statue and have accepted the mark of his name.'"

The Holy Spirit thankfully delivers a word of encouragement to those who will belong to the Lord in the Great Tribulation.

Revelation 14:12-13 "12 This means that God's holy people must endure persecution patiently, obeying his commands and maintaining their faith in Jesus. 13 And I heard a voice from heaven saying, 'Write this down: Blessed are those who die in the Lord from now on. Yes, says the Spirit, they are blessed indeed, for they will rest from their hard work; for their good deeds follow them!'"

John is about to behold a great reaping of souls, both to eternal life and damnation. Second chances are running out!

CHAPTER NINE

The Last 3 Angels & The Seven Bowls

IN THE CLOSING VERSES OF CHAPTER 14, THE SON OF MAN, THE LORD JESUS CHRIST, IS SEEN SEATED ON A CLOUD:

"¹⁴Then I saw a white cloud, and seated on the cloud was someone like the Son of Man. He had a gold crown on his head and a sharp sickle in his hand."

- GOLDEN CROWN--Represents authority.
- SICKLE--representing not a good harvest, but one of judgment.

What is about to take place with the appearance of the 4th angel is the answer to the prayers of the martyred saints who have asked for vengeance on their persecutors.

FOURTH ANGEL:

"¹⁵Then another angel came from the Temple and shouted to the one sitting on the cloud (Jesus), 'Swing the sickle, for the time of harvest has come; the crop on earth is ripe.' ¹⁶So the one sitting on the cloud (Jesus) swung his sickle over the earth and the whole earth was harvested."

This is the fulfillment of Matthew 13:40-43 where Jesus said, "⁴⁰Just as the weeds are sorted out and burned in the fire, so it will be at the end of the world. [41] The Son of Man will send his angels and they will remove from his Kingdom everything that causes sin and all who do evil.

[42] And the angels will throw them into the fiery furnace, where there will be weeping and gnashing of teeth. [43] Then the righteous will shine like the sun in their Father's Kingdom. Anyone with ears to hear should listen and understand!"

Notice that verse 16 shows that it is Messiah doing the reaping. "The one sitting on the cloud…" The fifth angel speaks.

FIFTH ANGEL:
The fifth angel appears from the heavenly temple also ready to reap a harvest.

"[17] After that, another angel came from the Temple in heaven, and he also had a sharp sickle."

On the heels of the fifth angel's appearance, the sixth angel appears.

SIXTH ANGEL:
[18] Then another angel, who had power to destroy with fire, came from the altar. He shouted to the angel with the sharp sickle, 'Swing your sickle now to gather the clusters of grapes from the vines of the earth, for they are ripe for judgment.'"

The *fire* over which the 6th angel has power is the fiery wrath of the end time. The 6th angel instructs the 5th angel to thrust in his sharp sickle.

The "vines of the earth" represents the false vine. Jesus said in John 15 that He was the "true vine" by which we are saved. No doubt, the vine the angel is addressing is the false vine of the Antichrist. Those who have followed him are about to be judged. It's the end time harvest where second chances no more.

When the 5th angel thrusts in his sickle, the Lord Jesus will tread the winepress of divine wrath. The Prophet Joel predicted this as well:

Joel 3: 12-14 "[12] Let the nations be called to arms. Let them march to the valley of Jehoshaphat. There I, the Lord, will sit to pronounce judgment on them all. [13] Swing the sickle, for the harvest is ripe. Come;

tread the grapes, for the winepress is full. The storage vats are over-flowing with the wickedness of these people.' [14]Thousands upon thousands are waiting in the valley of decision. There the day of the Lord will soon arrive."

The "valley of decision" Joel mentions is none other than the valley of Armageddon where the mother of all wars will take place. Keep in mind that this picture of "treading the grapes" is Old Testament symbolism. As grapes in the winepress were crushed by the feet of the workers, so God will tread down and crush His enemies like grapes.

John is now given a brief preview of the War of Armageddon that we will look at much more closely in Chapter 19. Here is the first sobering description:

"[19]So the angel swung his sickle over the earth and loaded the grapes into the great winepress of God's wrath. [20]The grapes were trampled in the winepress outside the city, and blood flowed from the winepress in a stream about 180 miles long and as high as a horse's bridle."

The War of Armageddon will be the war of all wars. So horrific will the carnage be that the blood will flow like a river up to the horses bridle (around 4½ feet deep) as far as 200 miles outside the city of Jerusalem. This seems incomprehensible, but if God's Word says it, it will happen.

The Seven Vials Of Wrath

As we begin Chapter 15, we see that John is once again transported from this horrific scene to one of splendor and beauty as he is allowed to see heaven. He witnesses a great sign and a beautiful sea of glass:

Revelation 15:1"[1]Then I saw in heaven another marvelous event of great significance. Seven angels were holding the seven last plagues, which would bring God's wrath to completion."

We have now arrived at the final seven judgments of God, making twenty-one in all. The word "wrath" John uses is the Greek word "thumos" meaning "hot fury." The Apostle begins with a stunning scene: "I saw before me what seemed to be a glass sea mixed with fire." (Revelation 15:2)

Again, we shouldn't let this symbolism intimidate us. The Bible is the best interpreter of itself.

- GLASS--Represented permanence to the ancients.
- FIRE--Is representative of something purifying. In this case it is righteous judgment.

Thus, the glass-like sea of fire represents purifying judgment with eternity stretching beyond. John continues: "And on it (the sea) stood all the people who had been victorious over the beast and his statue and the number representing his name."

These are the Tribulation Saints who have been martyred under the reign of Antichrist. They have refused to worship him, and have refused the mark of the beast. John records a moving and victorious sight:

[2b] "They were all holding harps that God had given them. [3]And they were singing the song of Moses, the servant of God, and the song of the Lamb. Moses and the Lamb both represent deliverance and salvation. They sang:

[3b]"Great and marvelous are your works, O Lord God, the Almighty. Just and true are your ways, O King of the nations. [4]Who will not fear you, Lord, and glorify your name? For you alone are holy. All nations will come and worship before you, for your righteous deeds have been revealed."

7 Bowls Of 7 Plagues

Following this glorious scene, the Apostle's eyes are turned once again to approaching judgment.

Revelation 15:5, NKJV "After these things I looked, and behold, the temple of the testimony of the witness in heaven was opened.

The "Temple of Witness" is probably where God remembers the death of the martyred tribulation saints. It's worth noting here how personally and seriously God takes it when His children are mistreated! John witnesses now the awesome arrival of the final 7 angels carrying the last 7 plagues called "the bowl judgments."

Revelation 15:6, NKJV "And out of the temple came the seven angels having the seven plagues, clothed in pure bright linen, and having their chests girded with golden bands."

These are very elevated angels, clad in white and gold, both symbols of purity. They seem to pause before the temple:

Revelation 15:7 "Then one of the four living creatures gave to the seven angels seven golden bowls full of the wrath of God who lives forever and ever."

The four living creatures are the angelic beings called Cherubim, and we first saw them in Revelation 4:6-9. Cherubim/cherubs are angelic beings involved in the worship and praise of God (Ezekiel 28:12-15). Prior to his rebellion, Satan had been a cherub. When one of the cherubs hands the seven bowls of judgment to the seven angels, there is an immediate reaction:

Revelation 15:8, NKJV "The temple was filled with smoke from the glory of God and from His power and no one was able to enter the temple till the seven plagues of the seven angels were completed."

So horrendous are these seven last plagues that the heavenly temple is filled with smoke, closing any access to this heavenly sanctuary—as far as John's view is concerned—until the seven plagues are fulfilled. This is it. The final curtain is falling. The final actors on the stage of world history are about to witness the end.

Revelation 16:1 "Then I heard a mighty voice from the Temple say to the seven angels, 'Go your ways and pour out on the earth the seven bowls containing God's wrath.'"

In Chapter 16, the seven angels with seven bowls are released from the throne room with the command to pour God's wrath out. The result of the first bowl is nightmarish yet all to real:

"²So the first angel left the Temple and poured out his bowl on the earth, and horrible, malignant sores broke out on everyone who had the mark of the beast and who worshipped his statue."

These sores are akin to skin cancers of the worst kind. Since John uses the word "horrible" translated from the Greek words *kakos* and *poneros*, meaning "grievous and evil." We might assume something like melanoma.

Next the 2nd bowl is poured out:

"³Then the second angel poured out his bowl on the sea, and it became like the blood of a corpse. And everything in the sea died."

When the second angel pours out his vial on the oceans, they undergo a complete change of chemical composition, whereas in the earlier trumpet judgment only a third of the seas were affected. This bowl judgment brings, tragically, total destruction to the oceans and all marine life.

Then the 3rd bowl is poured out:

Revelation 16:4 "Then the third angel poured out his bowl on the rivers and springs and they became blood."

The rivers and springs have now been struck, all turned to blood. As this happens, the "angel of the waters" proclaims the justice of the judgment, since multiplied millions of saints and prophets have shed their blood for the truth through the centuries.

We must keep in mind here that God's judgments are just. As Abraham said, "Shall not the judge of all the earth do right?" (Gen. 18:25, NKJV) The Christ rejecting, godless world of the Tribulation is only receiving the judgments they have brought upon themselves following countless warnings.

Revelation 16:5 "And I heard the angel who had authority over all water saying, 'You are just, O Holy One, who is and who always was, because you have sent these judgments. ⁶Since they shed the blood of your holy people and your prophets, you have given them blood to drink. It is their just reward.'" "⁷And I heard a voice from the altar, saying, 'Yes, O Lord God, the Almighty, your judgments are true and just.'"

Then the 4th bowl is poured out:

16:8-9, NKJV "Then the fourth angel poured out his bowl on the sun, and power was given to him to scorch men with fire. And men were scorched with great heat, and they blasphemed the name of God who has power over these plagues; and they did not repent and give Him glory."

It is stunning to see the hard-heartedness of last days mankind. John observes that, though they know these calamities are the judgments of God, they still refuse to repent!

These first four bowl judgments are devastatingly successful universal in their destruction of earth's ecology. The entire unsaved human race is smitten with cancerous sores, all of the oceans are totally destroyed along with all marine life, all of the natural springs providing fresh water are destroyed, and the ozone layer is obliterated (which might explain the skin cancers).

Though this could hardly be a more grim picture of the final moments of mankind on earth, we must keep in mind that it is darkest before the dawn. The Son of God is soon to return to install a glorious millennial kingdom of peace and righteousness! But we still have three bowls to go.

CHAPTER TEN

The Last Three Bowls

WHILE THE FIRST FOUR BOWL JUDGMENTS MIGHT BE EXPLAINED AWAY AS NATURAL ECOLOGICAL DISASTERS, the next three bowl judgments are such that no one can blame them on anything but the very hand of God.

The 5th bowl is poured out:

Revelation 16:10 "Then the fifth angel poured out his bowl on the throne of the beast and his kingdom was plunged into darkness. His subjects ground their teeth in anguish."

In Chapter 17, we will look much more closely at the rise of Antichrist's kingdom. But here John is jumping forward to give us a preview of how it will look toward the end. The fifth bowl spells the end of Antichrist's brief reign of terror. Apparently it is here that those who have followed him will realize they've been had. They will "gnash their teeth" in anguish over God's judgment. What a terrible place to be!

We see also that the 5th bowl is followed by a strange, cosmic darkness, possibly caused by dark clouds of interplanetary debris. The world is plunged into a frightening midnight. The 5th bowl especially affects the throne and domain of the Antichrist with this strange darkness.

Now the inhabitants of earth begin to recognize that this is the judgment of God. The kingdom of the Antichrist is coming apart at the seams. And what do they do? Once again, their rock-like hearts refuse to repent. Instead, of turning to God, they turn against Him!

Revelation 16:11 "…and they cursed the God of heaven for their pains and sores. But they did not repent of their evil deeds and turn to God."

Is there anywhere in the Bible where the wicked heart of men is more prominently displayed than here? Aside from Pharaoh's refusal to repent during the many plagues released by Moses, I know of none.

Next, the 6th bowl is poured out:

Revelation 16:12 "Then the sixth angel poured out his bowl on the great Euphrates River, and it dried up so that the kings from the east could march their armies toward the west without hindrance."

The sixth bowl judgment dries up the Euphrates River. Why does God do this? It is simply stated: "…that the way of the Kings from the East might be prepared."

God will make a way for the land armies of the vast eastern Asian continent to surge through the Middle East in route to the land of Israel and the final battle of the Great Tribulation. The enemies of Israel will march against her for one last, massive assault against the Jews. The final battle of that great day of God Almighty, the Battle of Armageddon, is about to take place.

Remember, the Euphrates River is 1,800 miles in length and 750 feet wide and 30 feet deep. With one sweep of God's hand its bed becomes dry ground. How this will happen is anyone's guess, but it is an amazing prediction!

These "kings of the east" will no doubt include the hoards of China and India, which are beyond the river Euphrates to the east. And we cannot omit the Muslim nations of Pakistan, Afghanistan, Iran and Iraq.

In this end-time scenario, God is bringing the forces of Satan across the dry river bed to be utterly destroyed by none other than Jesus Christ, Who will be followed by His heavenly forces, including the redeemed church.

The Prophet Zechariah also predicted this amazing event, "Thus the Lord my God will come, and all the saints with You" (Zech. 14:5, NKJV).

Jude quotes the Old Testament saint Enoch who foresaw the same thing: "Now Enoch, the seventh from Adam, prophesied about these men also, saying, 'Behold, the Lord comes with ten thousands of His saints, to execute judgment on all...'" (Jude 14-15, NKJV)

Notice in the next verse the "Satanic trinity" described by John: "And I saw three evil spirits that looked like frogs leap from the mouths of the dragon, the beast, and the false prophet." (Revelation 16:13)

FROGS were symbols of filth and dirt to the ancients. The frogs John sees are evil spirits that are energizing the unclean words of Satan, the Antichrist and the false prophet. And these evil spirits have a diabolical purpose:

Revelation 16:14 "They are demonic spirits who work miracles and go out to all the rulers of the world to gather them for battle against the Lord on that great judgment day of God the Almighty."

These demonic spirits perform supernatural, Satanically inspired miracles through the hands of, primarily, the false prophet. While the Antichrist is a political ruler, the false prophet will be a religious leader. Yet God is in charge of it all! Zechariah predicts in 14:2,

"I will gather all the nations to fight against Jerusalem. The city will be taken, the houses looted, and the women ravaged."

Notice, it is God who says, "I will gather all the nations..." He does this so that He can reveal His glory when He intervenes on behalf of Israel.

Next we see that, in the midst of these final moments in history, God makes a final appeal to the end-time believers to hang on; it will soon be over: "Look, I will come as unexpectedly as a thief! Blessed are all who are watching for me, who keep their clothing ready so they will not have to walk around naked and ashamed." (Rev. 16:15)

The "clothing" mentioned refers to their personal walk with Christ.

He's about to return and they will want to be unashamed at His arrival.

Finally, the 7th bowl is poured out:

Revelation 16:16-17 "16 And the demonic spirits gathered all the rulers and their armies to a place with the Hebrew name *Armageddon*. 17 Then the seventh angel poured out his bowl into the air. And a mighty shout came from the throne in the Temple, saying, 'It is finished!'"

With this final bowl, the *thumos,* or "hot fury" of God is complete. Startling signs follow: "Then the thunder crashed and rolled, and lightning flashed. And a great earthquake struck—the worst since people were placed on the earth." (Revelation 16:18)

Think about this a moment. Of all the horrific earthquakes to ever strike earth, this is the worst. This earthquake will not be measurable by the Richter scale. It literally rips Jerusalem into 3 parts:

Revelation 16:19 "The great city of Babylon was split into three sections, and the cities of many nations fell into heaps of rubble..."

It is a global earthquake. Cities all over the world will crumble like a house of cards! Suddenly, Babylon jumps back into the picture:

"...And great Babylon was remembered before God, to give her the cup of the wine of the fierceness of His wrath."

As already mentioned, we will look more closely at Babylon in Chapter 17-18. Where the full focus will rest on this end time city. John's description of the effects of this mammoth earthquake continues:

Revelation 16:20 "And every island disappeared, and all the mountains were leveled."

This earthquake—possibly the consequence of a nuclear blast—decimates the islands of the sea, perhaps through multiple tsunamis. And this awesome quake brings ALL MOUNTAINS DOWN!

Next, John observes something incredible and frightening: "And great hail from heaven fell upon men, *each hailstone* about the weight of a talent..." (Revelation 16:21)

A talent weighs one hundred pounds. A one-hundred pound piece of hail would be at least the size of a basketball! Though this seems impossible, history tells us that in the aftermath of WWII, atomic devices were set off causing the ocean waters to rise 30 to 60 thousand feet. When the boiling water began to fall, it created hail the size of basketballs. This hail was so huge and deadly that it damaged the ships placed in the lagoons, denting the ship's armor! Could it be that this is what John is describing?

The 21 horrific Tribulation judgments we've explored are punitive, not rehabilitative. Mankind at this point shows no interest in changing his ways. John yet again points out an unrepentant mankind continuing to shake its fist at God.

16:21b, NKJV "Men blasphemed God because of the plague of the hail, since that plague was exceedingly great."

While the seal, trumpet, and bowl judgments are complete, we are about to meet two mysterious characters introduced in chapter 17. Solving their riddle is going to be a real eye opener!

CHAPTER ELEVEN

A Beast and a Harlot

JOHN'S VISION OF THE SEVEN BOWLS PORTENDS THE END OF CIVILIZATION'S HISTORY.
But the revelation is far from over. We're about to encounter two puzzling characters John identifies as the Great Harlot and the Scarlet Beast. The Apostle is once again approached by one of the seven angels, who reveals a vision that astonishes him:

Revelation 17: 1-6, NKJV "Then one of the seven angels who had the seven bowls came and talked with me, saying, "Come, I will show you the judgment of the great harlot, who sits on many waters, with whom the kings of the earth committed fornication, and the inhabitants of the earth were made drunk with the wine of her fornication.""

The first lead character in this vision is a great harlot. The fact that the great harlot is sitting on many waters symbolizes a vast, worldwide influence. This harlot has corrupted the entire world.

Often in Scripture, harlotry refers to spiritual harlotry—a departure from the true God; or a false, apostate religious system. The constant refrain of the Old Testament prophets is rebuke to Israel and Judah for engaging in spiritual harlotry by their worship of idols.

This is what John sees--an apostate religious system working in coordination with Antichrist. We think of Paul's similar prediction of what will take place in the last days:

"The Spirit clearly says that in later times some will abandon the faith and follow deceiving spirits and things taught by demons" (1 Tim 4:1 NIV).

So who is this GREAT HARLOT?

She is comprised of an all-inclusive corrupted Christianity with apostate Protestantism, Roman Catholicism, and a blend of other false religions that produce one final last days' super-church. In light of the inroads New Age mysticism, false "feel good" Bible teaching, and other spurious doctrines that have infiltrated today's church, this is not at all difficult to imagine.

This last days' harlot church will look good on the outside, but shall be utterly corrupt on the inside. Antichrist will place his approval on and support it. Hence, the Harlot is in league with the Antichrist, which John introduces us to next:

Revelation 17:3, NKJV "³So he carried me away in the Spirit into the wilderness. And I saw a woman (the Great Harlot) sitting on a scarlet beast (Antichrist), *which was* full of names of blasphemy, having seven heads and ten horns."

The second character presented is a SCARLET BEAST, which is seen carrying the HARLOT. This beast has seven heads and 10 horns. We will look more closely at this beast in verse seven. First, more on the harlot:

"⁴The woman (The Great Harlot) was arrayed in purple and scarlet, and adorned with gold and precious stones and pearls..." (NKJV)

The harlot at first appears to be beautiful, richly dressed in royal colors, and bedecked with jewels. She is outwardly impressive. However, there's a very dark side: John sees that she "...has in her hand a golden cup full of abominations and the filthiness of her fornication." (NKJV)

On the outside she is impressive, but on the inside, she is thoroughly corrupt, filled with abominations.

Next, a third mystery enters the vision:

"⁵And on her forehead a name *was* written: 'MYSTERY, BABYLON THE GREAT, THE MOTHER OF HARLOTS AND OF THE ABOMI-NATIONS OF THE EARTH.'" (NKJV)

In Scripture, Babylon always pictures' rebellion against God, false religion, and the pride of man. It's genesis reaches back to Nimrod and the tower of Babel. The Tower of Babel was not built for the worship and praise of God, but was dedicated to the glory of man, with a motive of making a 'name' for the builders:

"Then they said, 'Come, let us build ourselves a city, and a tower with its top in the heavens, and let us make a name for ourselves…'"(Genesis 11:4, NKJV).

So, *spiritual* Babylon represents man's pride, rebellion, and the destruction that always accompanies a departure from God.

Next, John elaborates on the EVIL CHARACTER of the harlot: "I saw the woman, drunk with the blood of the saints and with the blood of the martyrs of Jesus…" (Revelation 17:6 NKJV)

Not only is the GREAT HARLOT evil in her influence, but is also literally drunk with the blood of the martyrs of Jesus. Her lips are stained with martyr's blood. John is stunned:

"…And when I saw her, I marveled with great amazement." (NKJV)

It Comes From Rome

You are probably wondering, "Who is this HARLOT? And the SCARLET BEAST that carries her?" John receives the answer:

"But the angel said to me, "Why did you marvel? I will tell you the mystery of the woman and of the beast that carries her, which has the seven heads and the ten horns." (Revelation 17:7 NKJV)

First, the angel identifies the origin of the SCARLET BEAST having seven heads and 10 horns: "⁸The beast you saw was once alive but isn't now. And yet he will soon come up out of the bottomless pit and go to eternal destruction." (Revelation 17:8 NKJV)

According to John, the Scarlet Beast exists, then disappears, then reappears again. John gives a clue as to what this means: "⁹This calls for a mind with understanding: The seven heads of the beast represent the seven hills where the woman rules." (Revelation 17:9 NKJV)

Most Bible scholars believe this is clearly talking about Rome, the famous "city of seven hills." The Scarlet Beast is Roman in its origin. John is telling us that Rome, the Rome that existed when he wrote the Revelation, would first exist, then disappear, and then reappear at some time in the future.

He is predicting a RESURRECTED ROMAN EMPIRE. Not the same buildings, laws, language, and so forth. But a resurrection of the culture, a resurrection of the *character* with which it is described in the Bible.

At this juncture it's time to pay a visit to the Prophet Daniel. It is very difficult to make sense of this part of Revelation without him. Daniel predicted the rise and fall of four world kingdoms, the fourth being Rome. He foresaw that Rome would be "…strong as iron. That kingdom will smash and crush all previous empires, just as iron smashes and crushes everything it strikes" (Daniel 2:40).

Let's look more closely at Daniel's amazing description of Rome. One day the Babylonian King, Nebuchadnezzar, had a disturbing dream that disturbed and perplexed him. Without knowing any details, God revealed to Daniel, not only the dream itself, but the interpretation. First, Daniel relates the details of the King's astonishing dream:

³¹ "You, O king, were watching; and behold, a great image! This great image, whose splendor was excellent, stood before you; and its form was awesome. ³² This image's head was of fine gold, its chest and arms of silver, its belly and thighs of bronze, ³³ its legs of iron, its feet partly of iron and partly of clay" (Daniel 2:31). The picture on the opposite page shows who those kingdoms were and when they ruled - three of them long after Daniel died!

~ Golden Age ~
BABYLON the Great
"the Lion"
Chaldean Dynasty
(634-562 B.C.)
King Nebuchadnezzar II

~ Silver Age ~
Achaemenid Empire
"the Bear"
Medians and Persians
(550-330 B.C.)
King Cyrus the Great

~ Bronze Age ~
Greco-Macedonia
"the Leopard"
Hellenistic Era
(336-323 B.C. / 168 B.C.)
Alexander the Great

~ Iron Age ~
Roman Empire
"the Beast"
Western and Eastern
(44 B.C. - 476 A.D.)
Reign of the "Caesars"

~ MODERN AGE ~
"NEW"
ROMAN EMPIRE
10 Kings / Kingdoms
(? European Union ?)
NEW WORLD ORDER

While this may all seem very mysterious, Daniel explains it:

"³⁶Now we will tell the king what it means. ³⁷Your Majesty, you are the greatest of kings. The God of heaven has given you sovereignty, power, strength, and honor. ³⁸He has made you the ruler over all the inhabited world and has put even the wild animals and birds under your control. You are the head of gold."

The head of gold was the king of Babylon. This was a compliment to King Nebuchadnezzar. Babylon ruled the world with an all-controlling, efficient, and powerful government for more than 80 years (625-539 B.C.). Even so, Daniel predicts its demise with the rise of another kingdom:

Daniel 2:39a "But after your kingdom comes to an end, another kingdom, inferior to yours, will rise to take your place…"

The next kingdom described by "arms of silver" were the Medo-Persian empire, which ruled the world for the next 200 years (539-330). But it too will come to an end, only to give way to another:

2:39b "…After that kingdom has fallen, yet a third kingdom, represented by bronze, will rise to rule the world."

The thighs of brass represent the empire of Greece under Alexander the Great (336-323) and his successors. After Alexander's death, Greece was divided amongst his four generals and was plagued with civil wars, eventually to be swallowed up by the fourth kingdom Daniel mentions:

Daniel 2:40 "Following that kingdom, there will be a fourth one as strong as iron. That kingdom will smash and crush all previous empires, just as iron smashes and crushes everything it strikes."

In vs 33 we find that the king's dream included information on the legs of this fourth kingdom: "…its legs of iron, its feet partly of iron and partly of baked clay."

The legs of iron represent the Roman Empire, which ruled from 30 B.C. to 476 A.D. (more than 500 years). The two legs were the eastern and western divisions of the Roman Empire, which came to pass after the fall of western Rome. Daniel continues:

"The feet and toes you saw were a combination of iron and baked clay, showing that this kingdom will be divided. Like iron mixed with clay, it will have some of the strength of iron. [42]But while some parts of it will be as strong as iron, other parts will be as weak as clay." (Daniel

2:41)

The feet and toes consisting of both iron and clay is a prediction that Rome would one day re-emerge, represented by the iron. Yet it would not consist purely of Roman culture, but would be a mixture of different cultures—multicultural.

Finally, Daniel adds one more thing that is sure to stir the heart of every Christian:

Daniel 2:34-35 "[34]As you watched, a rock was cut from a mountain, but not by human hands. It struck the feet of iron and clay, smashing them to bits. [35] The whole statue was crushed into small pieces of iron, clay, bronze, silver, and gold. Then the wind blew them away without a trace, like chaff on a threshing floor. But the rock that knocked the statue down became a great mountain that covered the whole earth."

The stone cut without hands out of the mountain represents Jesus Christ, the Rock of Ages, who will return to earth to destroy a one-world Gentile government headed by the Antichrist. As they say, in the end, we win!

John's main point is that Antichrist will rise out of a revived Roman Empire, and Messiah Jesus will ultimately crush his kingdom at the close of the Great Tribulation. The Revived Roman Empire is the 8th kingdom John speaks of in Revelation 17:11, NIV,

"The beast who once was, and now is not, is an eighth king. He belongs to the seven and is going to his destruction."

This EIGHTH KINGDOM will be the Antichrist's kingdom during the Tribulation. It will possess ten horns, which are ten nations that will offer their allegiance to the Antichrist:

"[12]The ten horns you saw are ten kings, who have not yet received a kingdom, but who, for one hour, will receive authority as kings along with the beast. [13]They have one purpose and will give their power and authority to the beast. [14]They will make war against the Lamb, but the Lamb will overcome them because He is Lord of lords and King of kings—and with Him will be His called, chosen, and faithful followers" (vs.12-14).

It seems very plausible that Antichrist will seize leadership of either the United Nations or the European Union, and that ten of its member nations will give their allegiance to him.

HAS ROME RETURNED?

The key point of Chapter 17 is the re-emergence of Rome—the SCARLET BEAST; and of the GREAT HARLOT—the apostate religious system that is carried by the beast and works with the beast to persecute and martyr the Tribulation Saints.

The Revival of the Roman Empire has, in fact, already begun in the form of the European Union. The EU started in 1948 through Belgium, Holland, and Luxembourg. From there it grew to ten nations with the addition of Greece in 1981.

It consists of more than 25 European nations as of 2015. The rest are associate members or have observer status. These statistics, of course, will fluctuate with time. But the prophecy of Daniel and John will hold true no matter.

Let's look at some uncanny characteristics of the European Union. First, the EU has chosen as its symbol a woman riding atop a beast. The statue below is located outside the EU office in Brussels!

Remember, John said, "...and I saw a woman sit upon a scarlet colored beast, full of names of blasphemy, having seven heads and ten horns." (Revelation 17:3, NKJV)

The depiction of the same symbol was reproduced on the centenary stamp of the E.U. and in a huge painting in the Parliament's Tower Building in Brussels. The photo below is the Second Election European Parliament postage stamp issued in 1984, depicting a woman riding a beast.

And below is one of the coins of the EU currency--again, a woman riding a beast!

The European Union is presently at the forefront of calling for Israel and the Palestinians to come to the peace table. It will be just such a peace negotiation, according to Daniel 9:26-27, out of which will come a seven year peace treaty orchestrated by Antichrist. The Prophet Isaiah calls it a covenant made with hell:

"You boast, 'We have entered into a covenant with death, with the realm of the dead we have made an agreement. When an overwhelming scourge sweeps by, it cannot touch us, for we have made a lie our refuge and falsehood our hiding place" (28:15, NIV).

But the prophetic word warns, ''When people are saying, 'Everything is peaceful and secure,' then disaster will fall on them as suddenly as a pregnant woman's labor pains begin. And there will be no escape" (1 Thessalonians 5:3).

The European Union's influence (Revived Rome) is currently growing at a phenomenal rate, and is clearly a candidate for Rome resurrected from the seeming dead. It may just be the Scarlet Beast with ten heads!

The European Parliament

The European Parliament is the parliamentary side of the European Union (EU) and has been described as one of the most powerful legislatures in the world. It has established a senior ranking high representative who has the power to call a council at any time, and to execute "emergency powers."

One actual document of the European Union is entitled "Recommendation 666." Recommendation 666 gives one person special emergency powers and the authority to act for the EU. At the very least, this is very interesting for any student of prophecy. Could Antichrist one day serve as the "one person" acting on behalf of the EU?

Physically, "The EU's new glass parliament building is out of the Space Age. The seats of its massive hemicycle (semi-circular) are designed like the crew seats in the Star Trek space machines."

The Tower Building houses the Fifth Parliament of Europe. The legislative amphitheater has 679 seats, each assigned to a particular lawmaker. For example (as of this writing), seat 663 is assigned to Rep Souchet, 664 to Thomas-Mauro, 665 to Zizzner and 667 to Rep Cappato.

Only one seat (again, as of this writing) remains unallocated and unoccupied; the number of that seat is 666. The relevant section of the seating plan provided to each Member reads as follows:

660 Marchiani
661 Montfort
662 Quiero
663 Souchet
664 Thomas-Mauro
665 Zizzner
666 -------
667 Cappato
668 Turco
669 Bonino
670 Pannella
671 Dupuis
672 Della Vedova

In 1999, Javier Solana became the High Representative for the European Union's foreign and security policy, and through Recommendation Number 666, he was given emergency powers over the military wing of the European Union in 2000. He has since been replaced. But the position is what's important. Will it one day be occupied by Antichrist?

All that currently remains to create a truly revived Roman Empire is the creation of a permanent executive branch of government and the full integration of the new Euro currency. With the introduction of the new European Union constitution, the groundwork is being laid for just such an executive branch and economic system.

The predictions of John's revelation are quite possibly being fulfilled before our very eyes. The Antichrist's seat will soon be occupied. The world primed for his full and final appearance. Ultimately, the Lord will destroy him by the spirit of His mouth and by the brightness of His coming (2nd Thessalonians 2:8). The coming of the Lord is near!

Yet John's not through. The amazed Apostle is about to view the complete destruction of a future city called Babylon!

CHAPTER TWELVE

Babylon Bites The Dust

A QUICK RECAP IS IN ORDER. IN THE LAST CHAPTER WE LOOKED AT JOHN'S PREDICTION OF ANCIENT ROME BEING REVIVED IN THE LAST DAYS, and that it would consist of a ten nation confederacy, or a "beast with ten heads."

We saw that this has already begun through the European Union of today, which began with ten full-member nations. This political entity may very well be what the Antichrist will seize and use in order to gain power during the Great Tribulation.

We also observed what John called "The Great Harlot." The Great Harlot is an apostate religious system pictured as a woman riding atop a beast. She will appear beautiful on the outside, but will be wicked and vile within. This Harlot is seen to be drunk with the blood of God's saints.

The Harlot will be the vehicle used by the Antichrist (the beast) to persecute and kill true believers. Amazingly, it is a woman riding atop a beast that the European Union has selected as their symbol! John's description of the Harlot carried on the back of the Beast suggests a demonic duo—one political, the other religious.

But their demonic union will not last. John ends Chapter 17 describing the fate of the Harlot:

Revelation 17:15-17 (NIV) "Then the angel said to me, 'The waters you saw, where the prostitute sits, are peoples, multitudes, nations and languages. [16]The beast (Antichrist) and the ten horns (ten nations in league with Antichrist) you saw will hate the prostitute. They will bring her to ruin and leave her naked; they will eat her flesh and burn her with fire. [17]For God has put it into their hearts to accomplish his purpose by agreeing to give the beast their power to rule, until God's words are fulfilled. [18]The woman you saw is the great city that rules over the kings of the earth.'"

The time will come (midway through the Tribulation) when the Antichrist turns on the harlot religious system, probably because he himself wants to be the center of worship. At that moment, the Great Harlot false religious system is utterly destroyed!

Just when the world is resting in a false security, Antichrist will break his covenant with the Jewish people, walk into the rebuilt Temple in Jerusalem, and desecrate it by declaring himself to be God. This event is what Daniel and Jesus both called, "The Abomination of Desolation."

Jesus warned: "Therefore when you see the abomination of desolation, spoken of by Daniel the Prophet, standing in the holy place, then let those who are in Judea flee to the mountains...for then there shall be great tribulation, such as has not been since the beginning of the world until this time, no, nor ever shall be" (Matt. 24:15, 21, NKJV).

This event will be the trigger point for the final 3 1/2 years of the Tribulation, which by far are the worst. The artificial security the world has been under will be shattered.

Babylon Reborn

Whereas Chapter 17 reveals the appearance of the Great Harlot—an apostate religious system, and her destruction at the hands of Antichrist—Chapter 18 depicts the destruction of a literal Babylon. This is where we witness the Antichrist system collapse.

There are two Babylons in the Bible. As already mentioned, there is first a spiritual Babylon—the apostate religious church of the last days. And there is a literal physical Babylon—a capital city accompanied by a system and culture that comes under judgment.

A literal city of Babylon will be the center of the Antichrist's world kingdom. Chapter 18 focuses on the social, financial, and commercial destruction of this last great government on earth.

Revelation 18: 1-3 "[1]After all this I saw another angel come down from heaven with great authority, and the earth grew bright with his splendor. [2] He gave a mighty shout: 'Babylon is fallen—that great city is fallen! She has become a home for demons. She is a hideout for every foul spirit, a hideout for every foul vulture and every foul and dreadful animal. For all the nations have fallen because of the wine of her passionate immorality. The kings of the world have committed adultery with her. Because of her desires for extravagant luxury, the merchants of the world have grown rich.'"

From Genesis to Revelation, the name *Babylon* has come up again and again. Babylon is referred to as a literal, physical "great city" more than once in the book of Revelation (Revelation 18:10, 16, 18, 19, 21).

Most prophecy scholars believe that the Babylon of Chapter 18 is an actual commercial city. Based on John's vivid description of her destruction, it almost has to be. If so, it may very well be talking about the Babylon currently located in Iraq. Have you ever wondered why Iraq has been such a source of intense conflict? Most people have no idea the crucial role Iraq has played in the Bible:

- The Garden of Eden was in Iraq--Genesis 2:10-14
- Adam & Eve were created in Iraq--Genesis 2:7-8
- Satan made his first recorded appearance in Iraq--Genesis 3:1-6
- Nimrod established Babylon and the Tower of Babel was built in Iraq--Genesis 10: 8-9 7; 11:1-4
- The confusion of the languages took place in Iraq--Genesis 11:5-11
- Abraham came from a city in Iraq--Genesis 11:31; Acts 7:2-4.
- Isaac's bride came from Iraq--Genesis 24:3-4; 10
- Jacob spent 20 years in Iraq--Genesis 27:42-45; 31:38
- The first world Empire, Babylon, was in Iraq--Daniel 1:1-2; 2:36-38
- It was In Iraq that Daniel was thrown to the lions, and where he saw the Lord in His glory over the Tigris—Daniel 10:4
- Shadrach, Meshach, and Abednego were also there and this is

where they were thrown into the flames.
- The greatest revival in history was in a city in Iraq, Nineveh--Jonah 3.
- The events of the book of Esther took place in Iraq--Esther.
- Ezekiel was there when the Glory of God was seen in its fullness by the Kebar River--Ezekiel 1:3
- Babylon was in Iraq.
- The book of Nahum took place in Iraq.

The Beginning Of Satanic Evil

So in Iraq we see the beginning of Creation, and the beginning of Satanic evil.

No wonder Iraq is on the world stage like it is. Is this not a place where our Lord in his Glory is still involved? Things began here; maybe things will end here.

Perhaps this is why such ferocious battles have taken place here, why there was so much resistance over its freedom, such hatred, such strongholds! Will Iraq actually be inhabited again? Yes! Will it flourish? Yes! Will it play a key role in end-time prophecy? Yes!

Many are unaware that in 1983, Saddam Hussein started rebuilding Babylon on top of the old ruins, investing in both restoration and new construction. He inscribed his name on many of the bricks in imitation of Nebuchadnezzar. One frequent inscription reads: *"This was built by Saddam Hussein, son of Nebuchadnezzar, to glorify Iraq"*.

As I write, plans are underway to rebuild the ancient city of Babylon. Members of the brigade's 2nd Battalion, 28th Infantry Regiment have escorted a group of U.S. heritage tourism experts to the ruins for the first of several visits to develop a preservation and tourism plan for the area. The U.S. State Department and the Iraqi State Board of Antiquities and Heritage have embarked on the preservation project, dubbed the Future of Babylon Project.

Joel Rosenberg, in his best selling non-fiction book, Epicenter 2.0 , wrote about the Bible prophecies in Isaiah, Jeremiah, Ezekiel, and Revelation that indicate the ancient city of Babylon in Iraq will, in fact, be rebuilt in the "last days" of history and become the wealthiest and most powerful city on the face of the planet.

But God has a word of warning to believers located there in the last days. He commands them to "come out of her" and "flee from the midst of Babylon, and each of you save his life" before He destroys Babylon (Revelation 18:4, NKJV; Jeremiah 51:6, NKJV).

John predicts that this great city, along with its culture and considerable financial strength, will be completely destroyed:

Revelation 18:4-7 "Then I heard another voice calling from heaven, 'Come away from her, my people. Do not take part in her sins, or you will be punished with her. ⁵For her sins are piled as high as heaven, and God remembers her evil deeds. ⁶Do to her as she has done to others; double her penalty for all her evil deeds. She brewed a cup of terror for others, so brew twice as much for her. ⁷She glorified herself and lived in luxury, so match it now with torment and sorrow. She boasted in her heart, "I am queen on my throne. I am no helpless widow, and I have no reason to mourn."

God is saying here, "Don't be misled—you cannot mock the justice of God. You will always harvest what you plant." (Galatians 6:7). John, therefore, lays out her doom:

Revelation 18:8 "Therefore, these plagues will overtake her in a single day—death and mourning and famine. She will be completely consumed by fire, for the Lord God who judges her is mighty."

It is clear that the catastrophe described here has never yet been fulfilled in ancient or modern Babylonian history. Three times the expression, "one hour," occurs (10, 17, 19), indicating a sudden and total destruction. The final capital will be consumed by fire in a short span of time, reminiscent of a nuclear inferno. Monarchs, merchants and sea captains are caught up in the holocaust destruction:

Revelation 18:9-10 "⁹And the kings of the world who committed adultery with her and enjoyed her great luxury will wail for her as they see the smoke rising from her charred remains. ¹⁰They will stand at a distance, terrified by her great torment. They will cry out, 'How terrible, how terrible for you, O Babylon, you great city! In a single moment God's judgment came on you.'"

The word translated "wail" means "a loud lamentation" as opposed to silent weeping. John shows the impact of Babylon's destruction reverberating in all the financial markets. There will be a total financial collapse:

Revelation 18:11-13 "The merchants of the world will weep and mourn for her, for there is no one left to buy their goods. [12] She bought great quantities of gold, silver, jewels, and pearls; fine linen, purple, silk, and scarlet cloth; things made of fragrant wood, ivory goods, and objects made of expensive wood; and bronze, iron, and marble. [13] She also bought cinnamon, spice, incense, myrrh, frankincense, wine, olive oil, fine flour, wheat, cattle, sheep, horses, chariots, and of slaves (the bodies) and souls of men!"

Last on the above list and most disturbing is "slaves and the souls of men". It has been estimated that one third of Rome's population was enslaved; and it was not unusual for 10,000 human beings to be auctioned off in one day in the great slave markets of the Empire. There were probably over 60 million slaves throughout the Empire, people who were treated like pieces of furniture, bought and sold, used and abused.

Is John suggesting that there will, in the end times, be a return to slavery? Maybe not in the ancient sense, but with sex trafficking and other forms of modern day slavery, this may not be too far fetched. With tyranny comes the devaluation of life. And tyranny will be the order of the day in the Great Tribulation.

Also, as people become more enslaved to luxury, with more bills to pay, they find themselves unable to break loose from the "system," which may well be the meaning here. Their literal "souls" are enslaved to this godless, Satanic world system.

It would take little imagination to conceive of a universal enslavement under the rule of "the beast." We have already seen that he required his mark on everyone who would buy or sell (Revelation 13:16–17), and he also demands that all people worship his image. He will promise "freedom," but put men and women in bondage (2 Peter 2:19). He will take advantage of the people's appetites (Revelation 18:14) and use their appetites to enslave them.

Hence, Babylon is a perfect description of runaway materialism, minus God. Look how quickly it can all be lost--literally in a flash! The description of Babylon's demise continues:

Revelation 18:14, AMPC "The ripe fruits and delicacies for which your soul longed have gone from you, and all your luxuries and dainties, your elegance and splendor are lost to you, never again to be recovered or experienced!"

What God gives, God can take away. Even Jeremiah prophesied of God's own people: "I will surely consume them. There will be no more harvests of figs and grapes. Their fruit trees will all die. Whatever I gave them will soon be gone. I, the Lord, have spoken!'" (Jeremiah 8:13)

Then next, John predicts horror on the part of those who traded with her:

Revelation 18:15-19, AMPC "The dealers who handled these articles, who grew wealthy through their business with her, will stand a long way off, in terror of her doom and torment, weeping and grieving aloud, and saying,

[16]Alas, alas for the great city that was robed in fine linen, in purple and scarlet, bedecked and glittering with gold, with precious stones, and with pearls! [17]Because in one [single] hour all the vast wealth has been destroyed (wiped out). And all ship captains and pilots, navigators and all who live by seafaring, the crews and all who ply their trade on the sea, stood a long way off,

[18]And exclaimed as they watched the smoke of her burning, What city could be compared to the great city!

[19]And they threw dust on their heads as they wept and grieved, exclaiming, Woe and alas, for the great city, where all who had ships on the sea grew rich [through her extravagance] from her great wealth! In one single hour she has been destroyed and has become a desert!"

All those who had profited from Antichrist's brief reign will mourn the fall of his system. Yet these merchants aren't grieving over Babylon's pain, but over THEIR OWN LOSS. It is a selfish grieving.

Then John reveals why this destruction has befallen Babylon:

Revelation 18:20,24, AMPC "Rejoice (celebrate) over her, O heaven! O saints (people of God) and apostles and prophets, because God has executed vengeance for you upon her!" 24 And in her was found the blood of prophets and of saints, and of all those who have been slain (slaughtered) on earth."

Remember the souls of the martyred underneath the altar in heaven asking how long it would be before their blood was avenged? This is God's vengeance on their behalf. Their destruction will be like Sodom and Gomorrah's.

Six terrible "NEVER AGAIN'S" are pronounced over Babylon:

Revelation 18:21-23, AMPC "Then a single powerful angel took up a boulder like a great millstone and flung it into the sea, crying, with such violence shall Babylon the great city be hurled down to destruction and shall never again be found." "²²And the sound of harpists and minstrels and flute players and trumpeters shall never again be heard in you, and no skilled artisan of any craft shall ever again be found in you, and the sound of the millstone shall never again be heard in you. ²³And never again shall the light of a lamp shine in you, and the voice of bridegroom and bride shall never be heard in you again; for your businessmen were the great and prominent men of the earth, and by your magic spells and poisonous charm all nations were led astray--seduced and deluded" (Italics mine).

At this point in Revelation, the political and economic system of the beast has at last been destroyed. All that remains is for Jesus Christ to come from heaven and personally meet and defeat the beast and his armies. This He will do, and then establish His righteous kingdom on earth.

Once again, John is caught up to heaven to view an incredible celebration and a white horse with a majestic rider!

CHAPTER THIRTEEN

The Rider On The White Horse

IN CHAPTERS 17- 18 JOHN HAS FORSEEN TWO BABY-LONS—A SPIRITUAL BABYLON, SYMBOLIZED BY THE GREAT HARLOT, and a literal physical Babylon that would become the headquarters of Antichrist and his evil political system.
—a spiritual Babylon, symbolized by the Great Harlot; and a literal physical Babylon, that would become the headquarters of Antichrist and his evil political system. Both will be destroyed. The destruction of the literal last days city of Babylon will be accompanied by the financial devastation of the entire world.

With the beginning of Chapter 19, the Apostle is once again taken up into heaven to hear a crowd shouting:

Revelation 19:1-2 "¹After this, I heard what sounded like a vast crowd in heaven shouting, "Praise the Lord! Salvation and glory and power belong to our God. ²His judgments are true and just. He has punished the great prostitute who corrupted the earth with her immorality. He has avenged the murder of his servants."

This incredible hallelujah chorus stands in sharp contrast to the wailing and weeping of the world over the fall of Babylon in Chapter 18. The four "Alleluias," or "Praise the Lords" proclaim the triumph of heaven, the judgment of the false and final super-church, and of the whole

Babylonian system, including the dreaded mark of the beast. The Lord has finally taken vengeance on those that persecuted and murdered His people. Remember their souls under the altar?

The 24 elders and four living creatures are now heard for the last time, giving a mighty shout of praise:

Revelation 19:3-5 "³ And again their voices rang out, 'Praise the Lord! The smoke from that city ascends forever and ever!' ⁴Then the twenty-four elders and the four living beings fell down and worshipped God, who was sitting on the throne. They cried out, 'Amen! Praise the Lord!' ⁵ And from the throne came a voice that said, 'Praise our God,

all His servants, all who fear Him, from the least to the greatest.'"

And then the voice of a great multitude, all of the redeemed of all the ages, sound out the final "alleluia."

Revelation 19:6-7 "⁶Then I heard again what sounded like the shout of a vast crowd or the roar of mighty ocean waves or the crash of loud thunder: 'Praise the Lord! For the Lord our God, the Almighty, reigns. ⁷Let us be glad and rejoice, and let us give honor to Him…'"

Following the fourth "Alleluia" comes the presentation of the Lamb's wife, the ransomed, glorified Bride of Christ in all of her spotless purity. This is the first of two suppers in this climactic chapter. It is the wedding feast of the LAMB and His BRIDE.

"…for the time has come for the wedding feast of the Lamb, and His bride has prepared herself." (vs. 7b).

Some have called this grand event the Marriage of the Bride, but it is here called the Marriage of the Lamb, because the bride is the Lamb— Jesus Christ's—chief joy. When all of the redeemed are around Him in heaven, then He will fully enjoy the fulfillment of why He died!

John notes the bride is dressed in white:

Revelation 19:8 "She has been given the finest of pure white linen to wear. For the fine linen represents the good deeds of God's holy people."

The "good deeds" of which John is speaking are the works done by

God's saints in obedience to Him. It is the deeds that are rewarded at the Judgment Seat of Christ, spoken of by Paul in 1 Corinthians 3:10-15:

"[10]Because of God's grace to me, I have laid the foundation like an expert builder. Now others are building on it. But whoever is building on this foundation must be very careful. [11]For no one can lay any foundation other than the one we already have—Jesus Christ." "[12]Anyone who builds on that foundation may use a variety of materials—gold, silver, jewels, wood, hay, or straw. [13]But on the judgment day, fire will reveal what kind of work each builder has done. The fire will show if a person's work has any value. [14]If the work survives, that builder will receive a reward. [15]But if the work is burned up, the builder will suffer great loss. The builder will be saved, but like someone barely escaping through a wall of flames."

So the "good deeds" for which these saints in Revelation have received the reward of "pure white linen," are works done in obedience to Jesus Christ. While good deeds do not merit our salvation, they attest to the authenticity of our salvation and are rewarded.

After the bridal banquet, the triumphant saints go forth to participate in the glorious appearing and the establishment of our Lord's long awaited Kingdom. Who is among these saints? They are identified in Hebrews 12:23. "You have come to the assembly of God's firstborn children, whose names are written in heaven. You have come to God himself, who is the judge over all things. You have come to the spirits of the righteous ones in heaven who have now been made perfect."

These are the redeemed of this age, rewarded and glorified, now ready to be exalted with Christ in heavenly splendor. Guests at the Marriage Feast will include John the Baptist, friend of the bridegroom (John 3:29), the Old Testament saints, the redeemed church, and the Tribulation martyrs.

The Marriage Feast will be a joyous celebration to honor the Lamb and the Lamb's wife before all of heaven. John is overcome with the scene. The Angel speaks to him again and says:

Revelation 19:9-10 "[9]...Write this: Blessed are those who are invited to the wedding feast of the Lamb...' And he added, '...These are true words that come from God.' [10]Then I fell down at his feet to worship him, but he said, 'No, don't worship me. I am a servant of God, just like you and your brothers and sisters who testify about their faith in Jesus. Worship only God. For the essence of prophecy is to give a clear witness for Jesus.'"

Any time we testify of Jesus Christ, we are prophesying!

Next, John witnesses the glorious appearing of Jesus Christ, the likes of which the world has never seen. In verse 11, heaven opens. From that lofty realm comes the all-conquering Christ.

Revelation 19:11-13 "[11]Then I saw heaven opened, and a white horse was standing there. Its rider was named Faithful and True, for he judges fairly and wages a righteous war. [12]His eyes were like flames of fire, and on His head were many crowns. A name was written on Him that no one understood except himself. [13]He wore a robe dipped in blood and His title was the Word of God."

We note next that the redeemed of the Lord enter the picture. The Lord Jesus's blood-bought saints return with Him. Even Enoch of old prophesied of this amazing event: "Now Enoch, the seventh from Adam, prophesied....saying, 'Behold, the Lord comes with ten thousands of His saints" (Jude 14).

John describes this spectacular event in living technicolor:

Revelation 19: 14-16 "[14]The armies of heaven, dressed in the finest of pure white linen, followed Him on white horses. [15]From His mouth came a sharp sword to strike down the nations. He will rule them with an iron rod. He will release the fierce wrath of God, the Almighty, like juice flowing from a winepress. [16]On His robe at His thigh was written this title: King of all kings and Lord of all lords."

Notice that His names thus far add up to six in connection with this majestic revelation. But another name, the Lamb, mentioned earlier in the chapter, makes seven names in all.

He is the Lamb, Faithful, True, Mysterious Name (no one knows but He Himself), The Word of God, King of Kings, and Lord of Lords.

This amazing event is the fulfillment of both Old and New Testament prophecies concerning Messiah's sudden and majestic return. It is a literal, personal, visible, physical, and spiritual return of the "same Jesus" who ascended up into heaven in Acts 1:11.

It is the event John described at the beginning in Revelation 1:7 "Look! He comes with the clouds of heaven. And everyone will see Him—even those who pierced Him. And all the nations of the world will mourn for Him. Yes! Amen!"

Horrific Armageddon

John's attention now turns from the vision of the mighty King of Kings, followed by His heavenly armies, the dressed in white armies of heaven, to an Angel standing in the midst of the burning sun. He summons the birds of prey, the scavengers and vultures, from all over the world to gather for "the supper of the great God."

Revelation 19:17-18 "[17]Then I saw an angel standing in the sun, shouting to the vultures flying high in the sky: 'Come! Gather together for the great banquet God has prepared. [18]Come and eat the flesh of kings, generals, and strong warriors; of horses and their riders; and of all humanity, both free and slave, small and great.'"

What are they eating? The bodies remaining from the slaughter of the armies of the world following the horrific battle of Armageddon. This gives us a sobering glimpse into the terrible punishment from the hand of God on this final generation. The kings of the east and combined western forces of Antichrist have gathered in the Valley of Megiddo for war.

Remember the four angels who were bound at the Euphrates River in Revelation 9:13-16? Their time has come.

"[13]Then the sixth angel blew his trumpet and I heard a voice speaking from the four horns of the golden altar that stands in the presence of God. [14]And the voice said to the sixth angel who held the trumpet, 'Release the four angels who are bound at the great Euphrates River.' [15]Then the four angels who had been prepared for this hour and day and month and year were turned loose to kill one-third of all the people on earth. [16]I heard the size of their army, which was 200-million mounted troops."

This massive army of 200-million men out of the east, along with the combined western forces of Antichrist, will be on the verge of annihilating the human race. Jesus warned in Matthew's gospel:

Matthew 24:21-22, NIV "²¹For then there will be great distress, unequaled from the beginning of the world until now—and never to be equaled again. ²²If those days had not been cut short, no one would survive, but for the sake of the elect those days will be shortened."

How will those days be cut short? By the sudden appearance of Christ Jesus! But in a mocking display of sin-crazed lunacy, the Antichrist and his forces, and the Kings of the East and their forces, will join together to fight the returning Messiah!

Revelation 19:19 "Then I saw the beast and the kings of the world and their armies gathered together to fight against the One sitting on the horse and his army."

King David prophesied of this stunning act of arrogance in Psalms 2:1-5, NKJV "¹Why do the nations rage and the people plot a vain thing? ²The kings of the earth set themselves; And the rulers take counsel together, against the Lord and against His Anointed, saying, ³'Let us break Their bands in pieces And cast away Their cords from us.' ⁴He Who sits in the heavens shall laugh. The Lord shall hold them in derision. ⁵Then He shall speak to them in His wrath and distress them in His deep displeasure: and fury…"

The returning Lord quickly deals with them:

"And the beast was captured, and with him the false prophet who did mighty miracles on behalf of the beast—miracles that deceived all who had accepted the mark of the beast and who worshiped his statue. Both the beast and his false prophet were thrown alive into the fiery lake of burning sulfur." (Rev. 19:20).

The Antichrist and false prophet are the first ones to break open the doors of hell, which is the lake of fire! This fulfills 2 Thessalonians 2:8 "Then the man of lawlessness will be revealed, but the Lord Jesus will kill him with the breath of his mouth and destroy him by the splendor of his coming."

The Lord Jesus, no longer the gentle Lamb, now appearing as the Lion of Judah, quickly disposes of the rest of the massive, end time army:

Revelation 19:21 "Their entire army was killed by the sharp sword that came from the mouth of the One riding the white horse. And the vultures all gorged themselves on the dead bodies."

It is here that the final chapter of man-kind's bloody history comes to a close. A glorious new era is about to dawn. The Lord will rule the earth! What an incredible vision of hope for a new day. And as we're about to see, Satan, the accuser, deceiver, and arch foe of God and man will pay for the agony he has wrought.

CHAPTER FOURTEEN

Satan's Ultimate Doom and the Final Judgment of Men

IN THE LAST CHAPTER WE WITNESSED THE INCREDIBLE MARRIAGE SUPPER OF THE LAMB FOLLOWED BY the mighty appearance of Jesus Christ to bring an end to the War of Armageddon. It is at this time He will judge the nations. Jesus spoke of His return and subsequent judgment of earth's inhabitants in Matthew 25:31-46, MSG.

He uses an illustration comprised of sheep and goats. The sheep represent the righteous saved, while the goats represent the lost. The distinction between the two is made by how they treated the needy, which Jesus presents as a way to authenticate their salvation. He says:

"When He (Jesus) finally arrives, blazing in beauty and all His angels with Him, the Son of Man will take His place on His glorious throne.

³²Then all the nations will be arranged before Him and He will sort the people out, much as a shepherd sorts out sheep and goats, ³³putting sheep to His right and goats to His left. ³⁴Then the King will say to those on His right, 'Enter, you who are blessed by my Father! Take what's coming to you in this kingdom. It's been ready for you since the world's foundation.
³⁵ And here's why:

I was hungry and you fed Me,
I was thirsty and you gave Me a drink,
I was homeless and you gave Me a room,

[36] I was shivering and you gave Me clothes,
>   I was sick and you stopped to visit,
>   I was in prison and you came to Me.'

[37]Then those 'sheep' are going to say, 'Master, what are You talking about? When did we ever see You hungry and feed You, thirsty and give You a drink? [38]And when did we see You a stranger and welcomed You, or naked and clothed You? [39]And when did we ever see You sick or in prison and come to You?'

[40]Then the King will say, 'I'm telling the solemn truth: Whenever you did one of these things to someone overlooked or ignored, that was Me—you did it to Me.'

Before we look at the fate of the goats it's worth noting that the saved sheep had not in any way sought their salvation through their good works. Their deeds were the simple outflow of having been genuinely saved. Those identified as goats bore no such evidence. Jesus continues:

[41]Then He will turn to the 'goats,' the ones on His left, and say, 'Get out, worthless goats! You're good for nothing but the fires of hell. And why? Because— [42] I was hungry and you gave Me no meal, I was thirsty and you gave Me no drink, [43] I was homeless and you gave Me no bed, I was shivering and you gave Me no clothes, sick and in prison, and you never visited.'

[44]Then those 'goats' are going to say, 'Master, what are You talking about? When did we ever see You hungry or thirsty or homeless or shivering or sick or in prison and didn't help?'

[45]He will answer them, 'I'm telling the solemn truth: Whenever you failed to do one of these things to someone who was being overlooked or ignored, that was Me—you failed to do it to Me.'

[46]Then those 'goats' will be herded to their eternal doom, but the 'sheep' to their eternal reward."

Let no one ever tell you hell isn't real. Jesus just described it!

The Millennium

As Christ returns and the Tribulation comes to it's terrible close, several things take place as revealed in Chapter 20 of Revelation:

- Satan is bound in the Abyss
- The first resurrection
- The millennium, mentioned six times
- Satan loosed for a brief season
- The last and final rebellion
- Satan consigned to the lake of fire
- The second resurrection and the second death

Verse one of chapter 20 opens with a special angel coming down from heaven with authorization to arrest Satan, binding him for a thousand years with a great chain and casting him into the bottomless pit, called the Abyss.

Revelation 20:1-3, MSG "I saw an Angel descending out of Heaven. He carried the key to the Abyss and a chain—a huge chain. ²He grabbed the Dragon, that old Snake—the very Devil, Satan himself!—chained him up for a thousand years, ³dumped him into the Abyss, slammed it shut and sealed it tight. No more trouble out of him, deceiving the nations—until the thousand years are up. After that he has to be let loose briefly."

The thousand years mentioned in verse 3 have been called "The Millennial Reign of Christ." This will be a glorious time when, as Isaiah describes, "The wolf will live with the lamb. The leopard will lie down with the baby goat. The calf and the young lion and the young fat animal will lie down together. And a little boy will lead them"(11:6).

During the Millennium, Satan is bound and chained in the Abyss for one thousand years. All satanic activity ceases, and all demon powers are gone from the earth. But what does it mean in verse 3 when it says that Satan is "let loose briefly"?

Apparently Satan will be released for a brief time at the end of the millennium to test and tempt the descendants of the survivors of the Tribulation to see whether their allegiance during the millennium is merely an outward submission to Christ's supreme rule or a heartfelt dedication to the Savior-King. More on this a bit later.

The thousand-year millennium is mentioned six times in the first six verses. During the millennium, Jesus Christ will rule the world out of

Jerusalem. And John says that the resurrected saints of this age and the Old Testament saints will rule with the Savior.

Revelation 20:4, MSG "I saw thrones. Those put in charge of judgment sat on the thrones. I also saw the souls of those beheaded because of their witness to Jesus and the Word of God, who refused to worship either the Beast or his image and refused to take his mark on forehead or hand—they lived and reigned with Christ for a thousand years!"

Notice that Tribulation Saints are also included--those who were beheaded for their witness and those who had refused to worship Antichrist or to receive his mark.

John goes on to tell us something else about this time period:

"⁵This is the first resurrection. The rest of the dead did not come back to life until the thousand years had ended."

The phrase "first resurrection" refers to those who are resurrected to enjoy the Millennial Reign of Christ. It will be enjoyed by three classes of people: The Old Testament saints, those caught up at Christ's return, and the Tribulation saints who are martyred.

Then John says:

"⁶Blessed and holy are those who share in the first resurrection. For them the second death holds no power, but they will be priests of God and of Christ and will reign with Him a thousand years" (20:6).

When John says that "the second death holds no power for them," he is talking about the resurrection from the dead of every person that ever lived throughout history and never repented. In other words, only the lost are involved in this second death.

It will be a "second death" for them because it will be a resurrection to damnation—in essence dying twice. They will be raised up from the dead (their first death) to face God at the Great White Throne Judgment (the second death). We will look more closely at this in verse 11.

But the millennium that the raptured saints, Old Testament saints, and martyred Tribulation saints will enjoy is what the prophets of old looked for, longed for, and predicted. It is what was on Jesus' mind when He taught us to pray in Matthew 6:10, "Thy kingdom come, Thy will be done on earth as it is in heaven." When He promised in Matthew 5:5, KJV, "Blessed are the meek: for they shall inherit the earth," He meant it!

In Revelation 5:10, the great chorus of worshippers in heaven cries out, "And You have caused them (the redeemed) to become a Kingdom of priests for our God. And they will reign on the earth."

Jesus promised a day of great reward at His return when He will say, to his own "...Well done, good and faithful servant; you have been faithful over a few things, I will make you ruler over many things" (In Matthew 25:23 NKJV). Luke phrases the same promise a bit differently, but glorious all the same: "...Well done, good servant; because you were faithful in a very little, have authority over ten cities" (19:17, NKJV). These passages clearly teach that faithfulness in this life brings authority in Christ's coming kingdom.

At this point many wonder what the millennium will be like. Thank God, Scripture has a lot to say about that wonderful era! Let's look at a few highlights:

- All things on earth will be restored.

Acts 3:20-21 "[20]Then times of refreshment will come from the presence of the Lord, and He will again send you Jesus, your appointed Messiah. [21]For He must remain in heaven until the time for the final restoration of all things, as God promised long ago through His holy prophets."

- Predatory, carnivorous animals will become vegetarians as before the fall.

Isaiah 11:6 "In that day the wolf and the lamb will live together; the leopard will lie down with the baby goat. The calf and the yearling will be safe with the lion, and a little child will lead them all."

- The glory of the Garden of Eden will be restored.

Isaiah 11:10 "In that day, the heir to David's throne will be a banner of salvation to all the world. The nations will rally to Him, and the land where He lives will be a glorious place."

- Christ will be the absolute Monarch, ruling with perfect justice.

Isaiah 11:4 "He will give justice to the poor and make fair decisions for the exploited. The earth will shake at the force of His word, and one breath from His mouth will destroy the wicked."

- Israel will be the preeminent nation on earth and will bless all the Gentile nations.

Genesis 12:2-3 "²I will make you into a great nation. I will bless you and make you famous, and you will be a blessing to others. ³I will bless those who bless you and curse those who treat you with contempt. All the families on earth will be blessed through you."

The Earth Repopulated, Satan's Last Stand

While glorified saints neither marry nor are given in marriage, the survivors of the Great Tribulation will do both, and will repopulate the world. They will live indefinitely in ideal environmental conditions in natural but super-healthy bodies. The Tribulation Saints that survive Antichrist's persecution will be the only candidates for repopulating our depleted world.

Isaiah writes,

Isaiah 65:20, NIV "Never again will there be in it an infant who lives but a few days, or an old man who does not live out his years; the one who dies at a hundred will be thought a mere child; the one who fails to reach a hundred will be considered accursed."

But a vast number of descendants of the saved survivors of the Tribulation will have only an outward allegiance without saving faith in Him. This is why, as mentioned earlier, Satan is loosed out of his prison at the end of the thousand-year millennium. He will amass a huge army and assault the capital of the world, the earthly Jerusalem:

Revelation 20:7-9, NIV "⁷When the thousand years are over, Satan will be released from his prison ⁸and will go out to deceive the nations in the four corners of the earth—Gog and Magog—to gather them for battle. In number they are like the sand on the seashore. ⁹They marched across the breadth of the earth and surrounded the camp of God's people, the city he loves..."

These foolish attackers are consumed by the fire of God: "...but fire came down from heaven and devoured them" (20:96, NIV).

Finally, Satan joins the Antichrist and false prophet in the burning lake of fire prepared for the devil and his angels:

Revelation 20:10, NIV "And the devil, who deceived them, was thrown into the lake of burning sulfur, where the beast and the false prophet had been thrown. They will be tormented day and night for ever and ever."

The Great White Throne

At this time, all the souls throughout the ages who died in their sins are raised out of the grave to stand before the Judge of the universe to receive their just and eternal retribution. Only the lost and the doomed appear here.

"[11]Then I saw a great white throne and him who was seated on it. The earth and sky fled from His presence, and there was no place for them. [12]And I saw the dead, great and small, standing before the throne, and books were opened. Another book was opened, which is the Book of Life..." (NIV)

If you're a Christian, your name is written into the Book of Life only and solely by the ink of the blood of the Lamb. There is no good work, no well-lived life, no claims to personal righteousness that can win you a place in that sacred volume. The moment you say "Yes" to Christ, your name is added. John relays the terror of those who must watch all their former sins brought into scrutinizing light.

Revelation 20:12, NIV "...And the dead were judged according to what they had done as recorded in the books."

When John records that there are "books" at that judgment, and that one of them is the Book of Life, another of the books is clearly a book of deeds. Every sin, every misspoken word, every evil thought and motivation, all wicked deeds done in secret will flash before you on that day as heaven's recorder recalls your life in a flash of time.

Revelation 20:13, NIV "The sea gave up the dead that were in it, and death and Hades gave up the dead that were in them, and each person was judged according to what they had done."

The "death and Hades" mentioned above serve as the spiritual waiting rooms of the damned. It is where lost souls go until the time of the Great White Throne judgment. They, too, will be judged:

"[14]Then death and Hades were thrown into the lake of fire. The lake of fire is the second death. [15]Anyone whose name was not found written in the Book of Life, he was thrown into the lake of fire." (14-15. NIV)

One commentator writes of the enormity of the word *whosoever*: "All persons, of all ranks, ages, and conditions. No word could be more comprehensive than this...All besides these, princes, kings, nobles, philosophers, statesmen, conquerors; rich men and poor men; the bond and the free; the young and the aged; the frivolous, the vain, the proud, and the sober; the modest and the humble, will be doomed to the lake of fire" (Barnes' notes on the Bible).

Where do you stand? Has the Son of God written your name in the Book of Life? There is no more important question. When we consider the glorious things John reveals next that God has in store for those who trust His Son for salvation, who would want to miss it!

CHAPTER FIFTEEN

The New Heaven and New Earth

A FTER DISCUSSING THE MILLENNIAL REIGN OF CHRIST FOLLOWED BY THE GRIM SPECTACLE OF THE GREAT WHITE THRONE JUDGMENT, WE STAND ON THE BRINK OF A BRAND NEW DAY.

The final two chapters of John's Revelation describe the Celestial City. John Bunyan called it, "the glowing and glorious capital of the universe," the place with heavenly dwellings Jesus has gone to prepare for His own.

As if he has taken a time trip into eternity, the New Heaven and New Earth are now unveiled before the Apostle's eyes. Forty times in the Revelation, John states that these were things that he personally saw.

Revelation 21:1, NIVUK "Then I saw 'a new heaven and a new earth,' for the first heaven and the first earth had passed away, and there was no longer any sea."

There will be no oceans on the new planet earth, no vast expanses of water, as now with island continents, nor a foaming sea of wicked humanity, which Isaiah spoke of: "But the wicked are like the troubled sea, when it cannot rest..." (Isaiah 57:20, KJV). John continues describing what he sees:

Revelation 21:2, NIV "I saw the Holy City, the new Jerusalem, coming down out of heaven from God, prepared as a bride beautifully dressed for her husband."

All things are created brand new. A genuine new creation occurs. John said, "The *new* Jerusalem…" Suddenly, a great voice speaks out of heaven:

Revelation 21:3, NIV "And I heard a loud voice from the throne saying, "Look! God's dwelling place is now among the people, and he will dwell with them. They will be his people, and God himself will be with them and be their God."

John sees that God will dwell with us, just as He did before the fall in the Garden. In fact, in the beginning of the Bible in Genesis 3, man loses his walk with God and the glories of the Garden of Eden. In the end of the Bible in the last two chapters, man's walk with God is fully restored along with the equivalent of the Garden of Eden. Man's history has now come full circle.

The saved of all the ages, including those people who are loyal to the King and do not yield to Satan's seductive last temptation we saw last time in Revelation 20:7-10, may live on the New Earth.

Next, John delivers a marvelous promise, one that I never fail to share to the bereaved in any funeral service I conduct.

Revelation 21:4, NIV "He will wipe every tear from their eyes. There will be no more death or mourning or crying or pain, for the old order of things has passed away."

The sickness, disease, sorrow and death ushered in upon mankind at the fall are gone now. Next, the voice from heaven says in John's hearing:

Revelation 21:5, NIV "He who was seated on the throne said, ""I am making everything new!"" Then he said, ""Write this down, for these words are trustworthy and true.""

And John did just that—he wrote down the final book in the Holy Bible we hold in our hands. The final words of the Revelation now unfold:

Revelation 21:6-8, NIV "⁶He said to me: "It is done. I am the Alpha and the Omega, the Beginning and the End. To the thirsty I will give water without cost from the spring of the water of life.

⁷Those who are victorious will inherit all this, and I will be their God, and they will be my children. ⁸But the cowardly, the unbelieving, the vile, the murderers, the sexually immoral, those who practice magic arts, the idolaters and all liars—their place will be in the fiery lake of burning sulfur. This is the second death.""

Overcomers, true believers in Christ, will inherit all things—all of God's vast and immeasurable riches. By contrast, all of the wicked shall remain forever in the lake of fire, which is the second death.

The City Of All Cities

From verse nine through verse twenty-seven an incredible description of the New Jerusalem is revealed to the old Apostle.

Revelation 21:9-10, NIV "⁹One of the seven angels who had the seven bowls full of the seven last plagues came and said to me, "'Come, I will show you the bride, the wife of the Lamb.'" ¹⁰And he carried me away in the Spirit to a mountain great and high, and showed me the Holy City, Jerusalem, coming down out of heaven from God."

From the top of a great and high mountain, John beholds the descending city. For the record, the famous "hall of faith" in Hebrews 11 is primarily a chapter that focuses on the saints of old looking for this city, and that is why their faith is commended.

Hebrews 11:13-16, NIV "¹³All these people were still living by faith when they died. They did not receive the things promised; they only saw them and welcomed them from a distance, admitting that they were foreigners and strangers on earth.

¹⁴People who say such things show that they are looking for a city of their own. ¹⁵If they had been thinking of the country they had left, they would have had opportunity to return.

¹⁶Instead, they were longing for a better country—a heavenly one. Therefore God is not ashamed to be called their God, for he has pre-

pared a city for them."

Some Bible scholars have surmised that the new city will float above the new earth, rather than rest upon it. Who knows? My own belief is that it will rest upon the earth. But it will be beyond description, however it appears.

John describes it:

Revelation 21:11, NIV "It shone with the glory of God, and its brilliance was like that of a very precious jewel, like a jasper, clear as crystal."

The city in which the redeemed of the ages will dwell shall glisten and glimmer with a supernatural radiance. It will glow with the glory of God like a jasper stone, clear as crystal.

Revelation 21:12-14, NIV "[12]It had a great, high wall with twelve gates, and with twelve angels at the gates. On the gates were written the names of the twelve tribes of Israel. [13]There were three gates on the east, three on the north, three on the south and three on the west.

[14]The wall of the city had twelve foundations, and on them were the names of the twelve apostles of the Lamb."

Surrounding the celestial city will be a wall of jasper, adorned with twelve gates inscribed with the names of the twelve tribes of Israel. And the wall will have twelve foundations bearing the names of the twelve apostles.

Revelation 21:15-17 "[15] The angel who talked to me held in his hand a gold measuring stick to measure the city, its gates, and its wall. [16] When he measured it, he found it was a square, as wide as it was long.

In fact, its length and width and height were each 1,400 miles. [17] Then he measured the walls and found them to be 216 feet thick (according to the human standard used by the angel).

Just how wide and how high this urban center will be is difficult to comprehend. It will be 1,400 miles long, wide and high. This is not all of heaven, but rather what Augustine called the City of God. Whether it is somewhat like a cube or a pyramid is a matter of conjecture, but it will have ample space for multiplied millions of the redeemed from all ages.

Since twelve is the number for government in scripture—twelve tribes, twelve apostles, etc.—this would indicate it is the epicenter of divine rule. John continues:

Revelation 21:18-20 " [18] The wall was made of jasper, and the city was pure gold, as clear as glass. [19] The wall of the city was built on foundation stones inlaid with twelve precious stones: the first was jasper, the second sapphire, the third agate, the fourth emerald, [20] the fifth onyx, the sixth carnelian, the seventh chrysolite, the eighth beryl, the ninth topaz, the tenth chrysoprasus, the eleventh jacinth, the twelfth amethyst. Talk about breathtaking color!

- Jasper--Is like light blue quartz
- Sapphire--Is deep blue
- Agate--Can be light brown or white
- Emerald--Is rich green
- Carnelian--Is flesh colored
- Shardony--Is milk-white with reddish strips
- Beryl--Is aquamarine
- Topaz--Is pale blue
- Chrysolite--Is golden yellow with some green
- Jacinth--Is a Gorgeous violet
- Amethyst--Is deep blue & red with flashes of purple
- Chrysoprasus--Is golden yellow with some green

As if that weren't enough, John describes the gates:

Revelation 21:21a "The twelve gates were made of pearls—each gate from a single pearl. And the main street was pure gold, as clear as glass."

Can you imagine gold so pure it is transparent? This is how pure the gold of the New Jerusalem will be. We will walk down a golden street you can see through! John continues with his glorious description:

Revelation 21:22-23 "[22]I saw no temple in the city, for the Lord God Almighty and the Lamb are its temple. [23] And the city has no need of sun or moon, for the glory of God illuminates the city, and the Lamb is its light."

No need for electricity, street lights, security lights, sun, moon or stars. For the glory of the Lamb literally lights up the city! And His light will illumine the world!

Revelation 21:24-25 "[24] The nations will walk in its light, and the kings of the world will enter the city in all their glory. [25] Its gates will never be closed at the end of day because there is no night there."

Because there is no more crime, there will be no need for locks or to shut the gates securely. Night time does not exist.

Revelation 21:26-27 "[26] And all the nations will bring their glory and honor into the city. [27] Nothing evil will be allowed to enter, nor anyone who practices shameful idolatry and dishonesty—but only those whose names are written in the Lamb's Book of Life."

The saved and faithful of the millennial age are brought to this New Jerusalem. None but the redeemed shall ever enter. Imagine a city at total peace with no fear of crime, no filthy pollution, no homeless and hungry, no need for law enforcement, no sirens, no shelters, no hospitals, no jails or prisons. This is the city of God!

Sadly, we're almost finished. But Jesus still has some very important parting words before we go. Let's enjoy together the last chapter of Revelation and of the Holy Bible.

CHAPTER SIXTEEN

The OMEGA

HAVING SEEN THE NEW JERUSALEM COMING DOWN TO EARTH OUT OF HEAVEN LIKE A BRIDE ADORNED FOR HER HUSBAND, John must have been overwhelmed at the things the risen Savior had shown him. He is now about to hear the Bible's final messages—the OMEGA (end) of Scripture.

Revelation 22 is the 1,189th chapter in the Bible. Without these final words, some may have assumed that the canon of Scripture was yet incomplete. It is not, and the angel is about to make that crystal clear. In the first five verses, John is treated to a scene of total paradise. It is perfect and serene, majestic and joyous. He first beholds a river flowing straight out of God's throne room:

Revelation 22:1, NIV "Then the angel showed me a river with the water of life, clear as crystal, flowing from the throne of God and of the Lamb."

So…there is a river, as the famous song intones. In an inspiration of prophetic insight, the Psalmist David anticipated this river: "There is a river whose streams make glad the city of God, the holy place where the Most High dwells." (Psalms 46:4, NIV)

John continues with his stunning description: "²It flowed down the center of the main street…"

The river's pristine waters flow down the middle of heaven's main street. And then, as if happening upon a long lost treasure, we encounter the tree of life, first seen in Genesis in the Garden of Eden:

Revelation 22:2 "…On each side of the river grew a tree of life, bearing twelve crops of fruit, with a fresh crop each month. The leaves were used for medicine to heal the nations."

The tree of life is a tree of healing for the nations. John sees it blossoming, growing, producing a fresh supply of fruit every month. The leaves from the tree are medicinal. They carry the power to heal!

Next, he assures us that all curses will be gone:

Revelation 22:3-4 "No longer will there be a curse upon anything. For the throne of God and of the Lamb will be there, and His servants will worship Him. ⁴And they will see His face, and His name will be written on their foreheads."

Heaven will be unlike anything we can imagine. We will live in an imperishable, resurrected body, where no sin or disease can touch us. Worship of the highest order shall continuously fill that place. All of the redeemed of the Old and New Testament eras will be the servants of God forever, continually beholding His face and reigning with Him.

John goes on to describe the heavenly city's amazing features by rehearsing what he's already mentioned in chapter 21 regarding the Lamb as it's light:

Revelation 22:5 "And there will be no night there—no need for lamps or sun—for the Lord God will shine on them. And they will reign forever and ever."

Final Words

Now, from verse 6 through the end of the chapter, John records his closing words, the last words of Christ, and the final words of the angel. First, the angel assures the Apostle of the truth of the breathtaking vision he has received:

Revelation 22:6 "Then the angel said to me, 'Everything you have heard and seen is trustworthy and true. The Lord God, Who inspires His prophets, has sent His angel to tell His servants what will happen soon.'"

Then the Lord Jesus Himself reiterates the certainty of the events prophesied, including His return:

Revelation 22:7 "⁷Look, I am coming soon! Blessed are those who obey the words of prophecy written in this book."

Finally, John delivers his own personal testimony of all that has transpired. He is understandably so overwhelmed at all that he has seen and heard that he falls down again as if to worship the angel, as he did in 19:10. And once again, the angel tells him to "worship only God."

"⁸I, John, am the one who heard and saw all these things. And when I heard and saw them, I fell down to worship at the feet of the angel who showed them to me. ⁹But he said, "No, don't worship me. I am a servant of God, just like you and your brothers, the prophets; as well as all who obey what is written in this book. Worship only God!" (Rev. 22:8-9)

In the Revelation's last chapter we find several powerful instructions for the church, along with some final dire warnings for the lost. First John is ordered to immediately distribute the contents of the vision he has received: Revelation 22:10 "¹⁰Then he instructed me, 'Do not seal up the prophetic words in this book, for the time is near."

Second, the angel seems to indicate that once the events in the Revelation are consummated, there will be no more hope of a second chance: ¹¹Let the one who is doing harm continue to do harm; let the one who is vile continue to be vile; let the one who is righteous continue to live righteously; let the one who is holy continue to be holy.'"

Third, Jesus again repeats to John the promise of His imminent return:

Revelation 21:12-14 "¹²Look, I am coming soon, bringing My reward with Me to repay all people according to their deeds." When the Lord says "soon," He means that once the Revelation events begin, they will take place with rapidity.

Only One Way Into Heaven

Jesus makes clear who will be able to enter the city and who won't. There is only one ticket in, and it is the blood of the Lamb:

"^{13}I am the Alpha and the Omega, the First and the Last, the Beginning and the End. ^{14}Blessed are those who wash their robes. They will be permitted to enter through the gates of the city and eat the fruit from the tree of life, and may enter through the gates into the city."

Then our Lord gives, not a comprehensive list, but a representative list of the kinds of sins that will rob people of heaven. Five sins are on His mind:

Revelation 12:15 "Outside the city are the dogs—the sorcerers, the sexually immoral, the murderers, the idol worshippers, and all who love to live a lie."

The unredeemed are recognizable by these kinds of sins. The practitioners of these transgressions, having refused to wash their robes in the blood of the lamb, shall find themselves on the outside looking in. They will apparently see heaven, but be unable to enter, as was the case with the rich man in Jesus' parable (Luke 16:19-31). Jesus spoke very clearly about this while on earth:

Luke 13:28, NIV "There will be weeping there, and gnashing of teeth, when you see Abraham, Isaac, Jacob, and all the prophets in the kingdom of God, but you yourselves thrown out."

An Everlasting Kingdom

The Lord Jesus again reminds us of Who He is, and for whom the message of the Revelation was given:

Revelation 22:16, NIV "I, Jesus, have sent My angel to give you this message for the churches. I am the Root and the Offspring of David, the Bright and Morning Star."

Our Lord is telling John that the promise to David, that his kingdom would be an everlasting one, is now fulfilled. The Prophet Isaiah, for one, predicted that Messiah Jesus would fulfill this promise:

Isaiah 9:6-7, NKJV "For unto us a Child is born, unto us a Son is given: and…of the increase of His government and peace there shall be no end, upon the throne of David, and upon his kingdom, to order it, and to establish it with judgment and with justice from henceforth even forever. The zeal of the LORD of hosts will perform this."

Likewise, when Mary was visited by the angel of God, she was told that the Son to whom she would give birth would be the fulfillment of this promise to David:

Luke 1:30-33 "30'Don't be afraid, Mary,' the angel told her, 'for you have found favor with God! 31You will conceive and give birth to a Son, and you will name Him Jesus. 32He will be very great and will be called the Son of the Most High. The Lord God will give Him the throne of His ancestor David. 33And He will reign over Israel forever; His Kingdom will never end!'"

And now in the final chapter of the Bible, the Risen Savior and Messiah, Jesus Christ, is announcing that He is the One promised!

The Bible's Last Invitation

A powerful and compelling invitation is issued to all who look for forgiveness and salvation:

"17And the Spirit and the bride say, 'Come!' And let him who hears say, 'Come!' And let him who thirsts come. Whoever desires let him take the water of life freely." (Rev. 22:17, NKJV)

The invitation to join in the blessing of what the Son of God has purchased with His blood is offered to "whosoever will." Jesus alone can quench the deepest thirst of the human soul!

The Bible's Last Warning

One final warning remains that has often come to me when preparing a message to preach. It warns all who would tamper with God's Word by adding or subtracting from it to think twice:

Revelation 22:18-19 "18And I solemnly declare to everyone who hears the words of prophecy written in this book: If anyone adds anything to what is written here, God will add to that person the plagues described in this book. [19]And if anyone removes any of the words from this book of prophecy, God will remove that person's share in the tree of life and in the holy city that are described in this book."

The consequences for trifling with the Holy Bible are severe. All of the [21] plagues—the seven seals, seven trumpets, and seven bowls—will fall on the person or persons adding to or taking away from Scripture!

The final chapter of Revelation and of the Bible concludes with the last promise of Christ, the last prayer in the Bible, and the last benediction.

Revelation 21:20-21 "[20]He who is the faithful witness to all these things says, 'Yes, I am coming soon!' Amen! Come, Lord Jesus! [21]May the grace of the Lord Jesus be with God's holy people."

While the Old Testament closes with the words, "...lest I come and smite the earth with a curse,» (Malachi 4:6, KJV) the New Testament ends with "the grace of our Lord Jesus Christ."

Even so, come Lord Jesus!

Biography

Born in upstate New York, **Jeff Wickwire** grew up in Dallas, Texas, after moving with his family at five years of age. At sixteen, after being arrested for drug involvement at the height of the hippie movement, Jeff experienced a dynamic conversion to Christ.

Since then Jeff has served in many capacities, including prison minister, youth pastor, college and career director, radio evangelist and, for the last 23 years, senior pastor.

Jeff graduated from the University of North Texas and continued his education at Luther Rice Seminary and Tyndale Theological Seminary, where he earned both his master's and doctoral degrees.

He has founded three successful, growing churches. He currently serves as pastor of *Turning*Point Church in Fort Worth. One of the earmarks of Jeff's ministry has been large numbers of conversions. Thousands of people have been won to Christ through the years.

Jeff is known for his practical, clear and timely messages that "put something in your pocket you can carry home and use the next day." His vivid illustrations and commonsense approach to Scripture are widely known for making Christianity easy to understand and live.

Jeff currently lives in Fort Worth with his wife, Cathy.

Jeff has written Making It Right When You Feel Wronged (Chosen, 2003), Gossip, Slander and Other Favorite Pastimes (*Turning*Point, 2005) and The Windshield Is Bigger Than the Rearview Mirror (Chosen, 2006).

For booking and/or product information please contact:

Jeff Wickwire
10700 Old Burleson Rd
Fort Worth, TX 76140
Email: pastorjeff@tpcfamily.org

"Getting stuck in the past is one of the most common battles that Christians face - and the enemy revels in it because it distracts us from God's plan. I am confident that Jeff Wickwire will help readers move on and discover the joy that awaits them on the other side."
--James Robison, president and founder, LIFE Outreach International

"The Windshield Is Bigger Than the Rearview Mirror is an outstanding, uplifting book! With humorous anecdotes and wise insight, Dr. Wickwire inspires us to embrace the hope found in our God-ordained vision and to release everything that lies behind that might hinder our pressing on to His perfect plan."
--John Bevere, author speaker; president, Messenger International

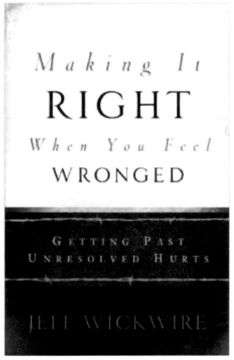

Making It
RIGHT
When You Feel
WRONGED

GETTING PAST
UNRESOLVED HURTS

JEFF WICKWIRE

"The Christian walk is one of balance, but Jeff is a high-wire artist.
Recommended reading for those of you trying to keep balance in your
life."
--TOMMY TENNEY,
GODCHASERS NETWORK

After twenty years as a pastor, Jeff Wickwire has seen over and over
again the devastating consequences of unresolved hurts - to churches
and to individuals. But he has also experienced the tremendous rewards
that come to those who handle offenses God's way.

You will come away from reading this resource with specific steps
to follow on the path toward freedom - freedom that comes only in
forgiveness, remembering that your future depends not on what has
happened to you but on how you respond to it.